EXTRA SPRINKLES

MORE REFLECTIONS FROM THE HEARTLAND

LORI LACINA

Lori
Lacina

First printed in June 2020
Printed in the United States
ISBN-13: 9781726228787 (paperback)

CONTENTS

CHAPTER III
FAMILY AND FRIENDS

CHAPTER IV
PLACES AND FACES

CHAPTER V
POTPOURRI

CHAPTER VI
ALPHABET SOUP

To Verne, the keeper of my heart.

Thanks for your unwavering love and support. You give me the courage to spread my wings, to seek out the next adventure, and the knowledge that you will walk beside me every step of the journey.

PREFACE

Dear Readers,

Welcome to my second book of essays. I can hardly believe I am inviting you to read my second book. Writing the first book was a lifelong dream, and as they say...here I go again!!

My first book, "Mama Said There'd Be Days Like This," was a daily reading of short essays, designed to entertain, motivate and inspire the reader. The essays in this book tend to be a little longer and are grouped by themes. The purpose remains intact. I hope you will relate to my stories, laugh at my antics, and reflect with me about our life experiences.

This title didn't come to me as easily as the first one did. Extra sprinkles can mean many different things. To me, extra sprinkles are the small moments in life that end up being the most meaningful in the end. A quiet conversation with a friend...that extra cup of coffee on a rainy day...twilight, when day slips into night...the joy of a child's laughter... and of course the extra sprinkles on your doughnut!

We only get one chance, as a spiritual being to have the human/mortal life experience. Grab that opportunity with gusto and hang on tight! Write furiously on all the pages of the book of your life. Fill them up! Scribble, color, doodle, imagine, love and laugh. One step outside your comfort zone, the adventure begins...start walking.

With gratitude,

Lori Lacina

ICE CREAM

SPRINKLES !

CHAPTER I

BOOKS AND WORDS

"I know nothing in the world that has as much power as a word. Sometimes I write one, and I look at it, until it begins to shine."

— EMILY DICKINSON, AMERICAN POET

HOW TO WRITE A BOOK

HERE IS a list of helpful hints in no particular order, in case you too would like to enter the world of authordom. It's a great place, but the path can be dark and lonely at times!! Bring a flashlight.

Scout a location for your office. Bookshops, coffee shops, the park, and the beach are all good locations. Keep in mind you can and should have more than one office location. It makes it harder for friends and family to hunt you down, and remind you about your real life.

Purchase printer paper in large quantities for cost savings.

Invest in multicolored note cards upon which to write your brilliant ideas. (Maybe it's just me, but it made it more fun.!)

Research what software you should use to write the book so you don't encounter challenges later...not that I have personal experience in this area. Then write, re-write, re-write, re-write and repeat!

Find a beta reader, a proof-reader, a barista, a bartender and an editor. Pay for professional help in the areas where you are not an expert. Polish the book with their help until it shines. Proofread, polish and persist!

Be prepared to have moments of excitement, vulnerability and intense moments of terror as you realize and hope that "random people" might actually read your words someday.

Don't tell anyone you are undertaking this project until it is well on its way and you have some confidence you can complete it. You don't need pressure from the outside world! The last thing you need is people asking you about it ad nauseam.

Enjoy the process. Have fun, enjoy the outpouring of your creativity. It is an incredibly rewarding personal experience and has changed my life.

Shannon Hale, Author and Newbery Award Winner said, "I'm writing a first draft and reminding myself that I'm simply shoveling sand into a box so that later I can build castles." Just start writing, get the energy flowing from your brain to the paper. Be not afraid to share your thoughts, ideas, and feelings. Get the words on paper, stream of consciousness style if need be. You can sort the wheat from the chaff later! Go forth and write and good luck!

RANDOM WORDS FROM A TO Z

I DECIDED to write a word for each letter of the alphabet, no thought, rhyme or reason. I just sat and typed each letter, and let a word come to mind. I invite you to add your A to Z list next to mine. It was entertaining and a brain exercise of sorts. It also could be a good writing prompt if one is staring at a blank page. Not that I personally know about that...

A-Algorithms	N-November
B-Bagels	O-Oblong
C-Comedy	P-Pie
D-Destiny	Q-Quizzical
E-Eternity	R- Resilience
F-Fire	S-Silence
G-Giraffes	T-Tambourine
H-Humor	U-Ukulele
I-Incidental	V-Vacant
J-Jabberwocky	W-Wise
K-Kitsch	X-Xerox
L-Lasting	Y-Yippee
M-Magic	Z-Zap

I am a self-proclaimed logophile, someone who loves words. I love the funny quirks in the English language, the meanings, pronunciation, alliterations, and most of all the way we combine words into sentences, conversations, and writing to share with the world. Never underestimate the power of putting pen to paper and expressing your thoughts and feelings. It is liberating, cathartic and creative. Tracy Chapman, an American singer/songwriter said this: "There's a power in words. There's a power in being able to explain and describe and articulate what you know and feel and believe about the world and about yourself."

A TRIP TO THE LIBRARY

I FONDLY REMEMBER my elementary school years and the joy that I experienced when my mom took us to the Public Library. It was a magical place, where they kept ALL the books! I was the proud owner of my own library card but consistently used my mom's. As a child, there was a limit on my card, which did not allow the number of books that I wanted to check out on a visit. I would leave there with a

stack of books almost as tall as I was. I loved books then, love them now!! I owe my mom a big thank you for introducing me to the joys of reading, which has given me a lifetime of pleasure.

Our library in Iowa City was a Carnegie Library and opened in 1904. A Carnegie Library meant that it was built with money donated by Andrew Carnegie, a Scottish-American businessman, and philanthropist.

Thanks to Mr. Carnegie, about 2,500 libraries were built between 1883 and 1929. I would like to have met a man like him, who must have shared my love of books and reading!!

> "A Library in the middle of a community is a cross between an emergency exit, a life raft, and a festival. They are cathedrals of the mind; hospitals of the soul; theme parks of the imagination."

> — CAITLAIN MORAN, JOURNALIST, AND AUTHOR.

Treat yourself to a trip to the Public Library nearest you. It will offer an absolute buffet of delectable words, ideas, and books. It expands the mind and broadens the perspective. The library is a vehicle to take you to places imaginary and real, to which you would otherwise never be able to travel. Buy the ticket, take the ride, over and over and over again. It is a trip beyond description and will color your world for a lifetime.

TSUNDOKU

IN MY FIRST BOOK, I mentioned this addictive condition that affects avid readers and book lovers. It is described as the act of acquiring books and not reading them. I am afflicted with this condition, however, I do eventually read them. Sometimes they just get ahead of me, the acquiring is faster than the reading!! So now I plan to demonstrate to you how this works by sharing with you the books piled on my nightstand...and my windowsill...and the wicker basket by my bed... So here goes!!

Unsolved- James Patterson
The New Girl-Daniel Silva
Dragonfly-Leila Mecham
Undercurrents-Nora Roberts
The Dirty Life-Kristina Kimball
Night of Miracles-Elizabeth Berg
Before the Fall-Noah Hawley
Sold on a Monday-Kristina McMorris
Born a Crime-Trevor Noah
Audacious-Beth Moore
Someone Knows-Lisa Scottoline
Fifty Things That Aren't My Fault-Cathy Guisewite
The Woman Who Smashed Codes-Jason Fagone
Warlight-Michael Ondaafje
Lillian Boxfish Takes a Walk-Kathleen Rooney
Scarlet Cinders-Martha Ann Letterman
A Reliable Wife-Robert Goodrick
My Twenty-Five Years in Provence-Peter Mayle
Maine-J. Courtney Sullivan
Oranges for Christmas-Margarita Morris
The Summer Guests-Mary Alice Monroe
Enchantress of Numbers-Jennifer Chiaverini
Women in Sunlight-Frances Mayes
The First Mistake-Sandie Jones
The Peacock Summer-Hannah Richell

Whisper Network-Chandler Baker
The Printed Letter Bookshop-Katherine Reay

I will stop now. This is the majority of the books...I may have left out one or two...accidentally. Allegedly, I may also have some pre-ordered that will be showing up. I hope by the time you are reading this, that list is decimated and I have fewer books taking up all the space in my bedroom. They taunt me when I glance at the stacks. That is not necessary and not appreciated. I will read them when it is their turn. I am reading as fast as I can. I have made a vow to stop acquiring more books until I get through some of these...except for the three I bought today...

Anna Quindlen, author, and journalist demonstrates my feelings very well in this quote, "Books are the plane, and the train, and the road. They are the destination and the journey. They are home." Yes, Anna, they are all those things and so much more.

Let a book take you on a journey, wherever it takes you, it will change you forever.

THINGS NOT TO SAY TO THE AUTHOR

WRITING and publishing my first book was an education for me in countless ways. Formatting, technical issues, cover design, downloading, proofing, and so many details I hadn't thought of. I sought professional help from those in the industry when I needed it, and the process was complete. As this second book goes to print, I am thrilled that some of the hurdles experienced before are much easier to complete.

I am learning yet more unexpected things as an author when people want to talk to me about my book. Keep in mind as I tell you these things, THEY are initiating the conversations. Sharing a sampling of some of these remarks...

Things Not To Say To An Author

1. "I saw your book at Prairie Lights and looked at a few pages but I didn't buy it." Okay, seriously, why would anyone say that. Stop after the words Prairie Lights and it's a winner.
2. How much money do you make on each book? How much money have you made so far? Again, just because it is a quantifiable product, why would you ask someone about their income. I don't ask you about your annual salary, Christmas bonus or your hourly wage. My new answer to this question is going to be simple, two words: Big money.
3. "How many books have you sold? Wow, is that all?" Do you ask your friend the plumber how many toilets he fixed this year? My new answer to this is going to be: I'll check with Distribution and Sales and let you know.
4. "Looked at your book, a good project for you, but it's really not my thing." I felt like a 2nd grader getting a pat on the head. Do not walk up to me and say this. Say nothing. I have lots of conversations daily that aren't about my book. Or say "Congratulations." Like my mama said, "if you can't say something nice, keep your mouth shut."

I might be a little overly-sensitive, but writing a book is an intensely personal experience. I am not selling candy bars, I am sharing and selling my personal feelings, ideas and stories. Some questions make me squirm and I don't know how to answer. I don't want to be a failure and don't know how you will react if I tell you how many books I have sold. The number would seem huge to some, and insignificant to others. I don't want to feel insignificant because I know how hard I have worked to write and sell this book.

Clueless, random comments do make me laugh...after the fact. However, at that moment, I am bewildered at what was said, and am trying to formulate a calm, measured response with particular attention to my facial expressions so I don't reveal how I really feel about the remark!

On a more fun note, the comments my eighth-grade students have are original, interesting and complimentary...in their way.

1. Has anyone famous read your book?
2. Have you had a lot of meet and greets?
3. Can I have a book for free?
4. Are you writing another book?
5. What do fans say to you when they meet you?
6. I'm going to tell my mom to buy it.

No, I am not trying to sell my book to eighth-graders in class!! They are aware of my book because their Language Arts teachers used a couple of pages for a book talk in their classroom. It is gratifying that they care enough to mention it and have some curiosity about it.

Writers need to write, just like artists need to paint or teachers need to teach. It is therapeutic, healing, calming and gratifying. Just the writing; not the book, not the selling, not the conversations, just the writing is what we need to do.

"Because creating something that didn't exist before is as close to magic as I'll ever get."

— FROM WHY-I-WRITE.TUMBLR.COM

LITTLE WOMEN — THE EPITOME OF ENDURANCE

I HAVE WRITTEN about the book "Little Women," on several occasions. This novel written in 1869 by Louisa May Alcott has incredible staying power. As I write this story, in 2019, 150 years later, another movie re-make of this timeless story is about to be released, with some big-name actresses as cast members.

"Little Women" has been made as a movie at least eight times, beginning in 1917. Katharine Hepburn, June Allyson, Elizabeth Taylor, Janet Leigh. Winona Ryder, Susan Sarandon, Christian Bale, and Peter Lawford have all been in this movie in its various versions. It has been a Broadway play and a musical. It has been an opera, a ballet, a show on Masterpiece Theater, a 2 part-TV show, and an animated version in Japan.

The latest version which just premiered as I am writing this stars Meryl Streep, Emma Watson, and Laura Dern to name a few. It is a beautiful film, and the best movie version of this iconic book that I have seen. It is true to the story and spirit of the book.

The story seems to transcend generations, societal changes, and modern technology. It is a coming of age story. It is the story of sisters. It is a story of war and hardships. It is an American story.

On a recent trip to Boston, my love of this story took us out of town to another historic site, Concord, Massachusetts, where the Revolutionary War began. However, my interest in the town centered around Orchard House, the place where this iconic novel was written.

Orchard House is historically significant because no one lived here after the Alcotts moved. The house is filled with their actual possessions. Louisa's bedroom (a/k/a Jo March) and the desk where she did much of her writing is just as she left it. It was an amazing experience for me to walk through the rooms and see the places that were written about in the book. I will probably go back someday but I am grateful that I had the opportunity once to see it

I spent some time in the inevitable gift shop that is part of these historic places. I purchased a couple of beautiful versions of the book. I do have a small confession to make. I wanted to leave my book, "Mama Said There'd Be Days Like This" in the home of a writer who inspired me so much. I really wanted to leave it in Louisa's bedroom, under a table or something, but the docents were extremely watchful. I didn't want to steal something, I wanted to leave something!! So, I settled for second best, and slipped a signed copy of my book behind some others in the gift shop, for someone to find.

When telling this story to my friend Sue, who has many times been a willing accomplice in my escapades, she said, "This may be one of your best yet." I must say, I giggle a little when I think about it. It was a harmless stunt but meaningful to me. My words together with her words. Mind-boggling!!!

I want to share a couple of quotes from the author that are my favorites.

> "I want to do something splendid...something heroic or wonderful that won't be forgotten after I am dead...I think I shall write books."

> "Love is a flower that grows in any soil, works its sweet miracles undaunted by autumn frost or winter snow, blooming fair and fragrant all the year, and blessing those who give and those who receive."

> "We all have our own life to pursue, our own kind of dream to be weaving, and we all have the power to make wishes come true, as long as we keep believing."

Well done, Miss Alcott. Your words are wonderful, wise and are thriving these many years since your death. Brava!

DO-NUT BOTHER THE WRITER

I AM SITTING at a coffee shop writing, which has become a weekly habit. The first hour normally includes coffee of some type. Today, it was just plain old coffee. Now, with two hours under my belt, I am having iced green tea and a multigrain toasted bagel with cream cheese. This is the typical sequence of fuel for my body and brain during a writing session. The ritual is important for my writing. However, the calories and carbs in the bagel may not be as healthy for me as I would like to think.

My most significant other, Verne, asked the all-important question; to which he had obviously given much serious thought: "Why would you eat a bagel when a donut is better and has fewer calories?" I found this somewhat personal question to be hurtful and unnecessary. I am very fond of my multigrain bagel when working. Besides, Mr. Smarty-Pants, they don't have donuts at the coffee shop. Donuts are not serious food, and when I am working, serious is the name of the game. Do not disturb the genius at work...or me either for that matter.

Donuts are just an excuse to eat dessert for breakfast. Don't get me wrong, I love a maple glazed donut as much as the next person, but there is a time and place for that frivolity.

To quote David Pinkwater, Author, "I've said this before, and I'll say it again. Bagels can be an enormous power for good or evil. It is up to us to decide how we will use them."

I have chosen to use my power for good, so keep the bagels coming and don't forget my cream cheese.

TEN WORDS

Sunrise: orange, pink, red, spectacular, hopeful, inspiring, beautiful, awe-inspiring, recurring, healing

Snow: crunchy, crisp, refreshing, cold, wonderful, shoveling, white Christmas, quiet, sledding

New babies: adorable, talcum powder, snuggly, miracle, huggable, sweet, kissable, beginnings, needy, diapers

Mashed potatoes: soft, fluffy, buttery, comforting, steaming, peeling, gravy, family dinner, grandma, home

Books: travel, mystery, romance, facts, excitement, new smell, bookmarks, relaxing, anticipatory, contentment

Music: memories, background, driving, singing, listening, stories, Christmas, change, culture, inspirational

Coffee: warm, iced, hot, flavors, pick-me-up, ritual, routine, cream, milky, steamy

Lists: to-do, organized, details, planning, annoying, helpful, shopping, chores, necessary, productive

Just acting on a whim today, trying some word association as a fun exercise to think of ten words that describe random subjects. You could make it into a family game, comparing how many words are the same on everybody's lists. I also find it helpful when I am trying to brainstorm. Just another symptom of my incurable malady that is my love of words!

NON-HYPHENATED

THIS STORY IS for those who wonder about my fascination and love of words, and the vagaries of the English language. The hyphen is probably the most under-appreciated punctuation mark in our language. It separates words, yet at the same time combining them into one. I am wild about the fact that hyphenated isn't a hyphenated word, and that non-hyphenated is hyphenated. I can't make this stuff up!! Well, I could, but some of you would catch me at it!!

Since I am in the "H" part of my brain, I have some other favorite English language phenomenons that begin with "H." These are types of specific words.

Homonym	Homophone	Heteronym
Sound-alike or	Sound-alike	Sound different
Spelled alike	Spelled same or not	Spelled alike
Different meaning	Different meaning	Different meaning

Examples of Homonyms: To, two, too
Examples of Homophones: Rose (the flower), rose (past tense of rise), Carat, carrot
Examples of Heteronyms: Bow (on a gift), bow (forward part of a boat),

If you are totally confused, you should have seen me trying to sort this out to write this. After much head-scratching, I think a word can

be all three things. I could be wrong. I think I will hyphenate some words to unwind. I might need to find a different obsession, maybe colors, how hard could that be?

I like red...cherry, rose, garnet, burgundy, brick, cinnamon, rust, maroon, scarlet, blush, sangria...Okay, maybe I will stick with words...for now. Unless I can find some colors to hyphenate...

THE LORD'S PRAYER — NO ALTERATIONS NEEDED

IT SEEMS TO ME, there are some things that should be left alone. I am always up for change if it makes sense, is an improvement, or lightens the workload. However, QUIT changing things that don't require change!! I have been saying the Lord's Prayer since I was a child.

The words are comforting and familiar. They are meaningful to me.

I recently attended a local church of the same denomination of my "home church." The words to the Lord's Prayer were different in what I found to be a very significant way. So much so, that in the worship guide, the words to the prayer were printed, with a disclaimer that the individual worshiper could say whatever words to the prayer that made them "comfortable." What?? I attempted to say the words to the prayer as I had learned them, but it is disruptive and distracting when others are saying them in the different, printed version.

There is a certain rhythm and rote to saying this traditional prayer, not unlike a chant, that is part of the beauty of it for me. To me, the church is a place of peace, ritual, fellowship, and comfort. Some time-honored rituals and traditions need to be maintained. Are we going to change the song "Amazing Grace" to "Amazing Divine Influence?" Change for the sake of change is wasted energy and upsetting to folks like me, who are still upset about Pluto not being a planet anymore, and this is way more important!!

Martin Luther said, "To be a Christian without prayer is no more possible than to be alive without breathing." So pray we must, and in the spirit of acceptance, I will pray with words that are meaningful to me, and I will welcome your prayers with words that you choose.

HISTORICAL FICTION

I HAVE FOUND myself avidly reading historical fiction lately, particularly those novels that take place during WWII. The stories are powerful, tragedy, triumph, survival, love, and loss. I wanted to share some titles with you in case you find yourself wanting to read something in this genre.

Dragonfly - Leila Mecham
Karolina's Twins - Ronald H. Balson
The Runaway Children - Sandy Taylor
We Were the Lucky Ones - Georgia Hunter (Based on a true story)
Lilac Girls - Martha Hall Kelly
Beneath a Scarlet Sky - Mark Sullivan
The Winemakers Wife - Kristin Harmel
We Must Be Brave - Frances Liardet
The Tuscan Child - Rhys Bowen
The German Girl - Armando Lucas Correq
The Flight Girls - Noelle Salazai

There are so many reasons I am drawn to these stories. The dramatic and unexpected bombing of Pearl Harbor is a historic event that changed the world forever. The brave young men that stormed the beach at Normandy on D-Day, who would become part of the Greatest Generation, inspire me. The Resistance groups all over Europe who fought the Nazi domination in secret at the risk of their own lives give me hope that in the darkest of times when all hope seems lost, that brave men and women will work together to overcome evil. The heroic men and women who worked alone or with a network to hide Jewish families to keep them safe make me marvel at their compassion and bravery.

The Normandy Cemetery and Memorial in Europe was the first American cemetery on European soil. The millions of visitors that come here every year to honor the brave men who sacrificed their lives are considered to be on American soil when they are in the cemetery.

" "You are about to embark on the greatest crusade toward which we have striven these many months. The eyes of the world are upon you...I have full confidence in your courage, your devotion to duty and skill in battle."

— GENERAL DWIGHT D. EISENHOWER, JUNE 6, 1944

General Eisenhower's confidence in these soldiers was well placed. They demonstrated all of the attributes he described, and we honor them still today, and forever for their sacrifices and contributions to the task they were given, the bravery they demonstrated and the cause for which they fought. Thank you hardly seems enough.

AN IMPORTANT BOOK

DURING MY LIFETIME, I have encountered many books that have been important to me, in a variety of ways. As much as I loved them, and love books in general, "My Important Book" may be in a category that is and will remain undefinable.

As children in early grade school, our television viewing was limited and controlled by our mother. We were, however, allowed to watch a very special program when we got home from school every day. I can still picture the three of us now, lined up, sitting cross-legged in front of the television set with eager anticipation of what was to come at 4:00 pm. Life was simpler then, there were not lots of viewing options for children, so this was a big event, every school day!

Are you ready? We were waiting for the Dr. Max Show. Dr. Max was not a doctor as far as I know. He was a kindly looking gentleman with glasses and a mustache who talked to us from the television, told us stories, showed us cartoons and generally entertained us. He also talked about books, and as an avid young reader that was great for me. He had a co-host/sidekick named Mombo. Mombo was a clown who would try to befuddle Dr. Max with his magic tricks.

Another feature of the show, rather like breaking news, was the Measles List and the Chickenpox List. Dr. Max would read the names of children who were afflicted with these childhood illnesses. I assume their parents sent or called in the names. I don't think our mom ever called in our names, much to my despair. Having your name read on the Dr. Max show would have been the ultimate in attaining fame and glory for us.

Now, for the best part...every year, Dr. Max created "My Important Book." I don't remember if it cost anything, but I am sure you had to send in to request one. I can still remember waiting so excitedly until it arrived in the mail. I was in heaven with this new book. It may have been the start of the many diaries and journals I kept over the years. The book was a small, pocket-sized book but it was chock full of many treasures! It contained games, poems, dot-to-dot pictures, blank pages for autographs or to write on. As you may imagine, I thought that I had many important things to do in "My Important Book!"

This book is such a strong memory for me from my childhood. When I think of it, I can picture my house, yard, mailbox, and myself as a young, gawky girl waiting for that treasure to arrive. These memories evoke feelings so strong, it is if I am living that time again.

> "Some days I wish I could go back in life. Not to change anything, but to feel a few things twice."
>
> — SOURCE UNKNOWN

I hope you have some of these memories and can pull them out and look at them at times. Write them down, share them with your family and you all will be the richer for having done so.

MEG — AN UNCELEBRATED HEROINE

I OFTEN WRITE of fictional characters who were my role models/heroines when I was a young girl. Typically, I think of Jo March from "Little Women," and Nancy Drew, girl detective. There is another book, however, that I have read and reread many times as a girl and as an adult that also has a heroine. "A Wrinkle in Time," by Madeleine L'Engle is that book. Before you even dive into the book, the title of the book is divine to contemplate!! As you may have assumed, hearing the title, the book falls into the fantasy genre.

There are many flashier characters in the book, but none more steadfast and heroic than Meg Murry. Meg is the 12-year-old daughter of brilliant scientists. She wears braces, is very plain (in comparison to her gorgeous mother) and doesn't fit in at school. At this point, I could be describing many 12 old girls!! There is something special inside Meg, that is very powerful. It is the reason that only she can rescue her father, and will face grave danger in doing so.

Meg's father, Mr. Murry (I don't believe we ever learn his first name in the book) is a physicist on a possible break-through scientific mission, and has ended up behind "the shadow." Yes, he has gone over to the dark side, but in this case, not by choice. He is a prisoner.

Meg's job, which she is thrust into, is to rescue her father. She is the type of character who is the uncelebrated, atypical, unwilling but stoic heroine. She doesn't choose to take on this role but is forced into being the rescuer. I think the reason I like Meg is she represents so many women throughout time and even today. The women who soldier through tough times, take heroic actions and do what has to be done; quietly and competently without parades and recognition. These women do not seek the limelight or bask in it if it shines on them. They face adversity, gather the strength within them and quietly go about changing their lives and the lives they touch. No muss, no fuss. I know many of these women. I admire their courage, their willingness to fight or advocate for themselves and others. They make the world a better place because they exist. They are the women who say, "I am fine," as they wipe the tears from their eyes and move on to the next mountain they need to move.

Let us all do a better job of celebrating the women in our lives for what they give to us and to the world.

 "She is clothed with strength and dignity and laughs without fear of the future."

— Proverbs 31:25

NEW AND IMPROVED WORDS!

OH, Happy Day!! Much to my delight, I discovered a website that promotes the creation of new, positive words. If you read my previous book, "Mama Said There'd Be Days Like These," you will already know about my not so secret love affair with words. The knowledge that somewhere out there in the great unknown, smart people are creating new words!! It's not like I already know ALL the words, and need some new ones. I do find great pleasure in sprinkling my writing and conversation with new words I have learned, or words that are very descriptive and are not used enough in my humble opinion.

The website was "Positive Words Research." Sounds like a place I would like to apply for a job. If I wanted a job, which I don't. Structured hours in which to ply my trade or any trade have lost their appeal as I have gotten older and wiser. Here are some of my favorite words that appeared on the list:

Up-leveled
Vocabuleverage
Funology
Positude
Earthing
Jubilingo

You can probably come up with most of the meanings of the above words, just by reading them. If one stumps you, visit your favorite search engine and look for it. I challenge you to use one of these sparkly words as you go about life today!! I also challenge you to climb a tree or run through a sprinkler but guessing you won't do that, so humor me and use the words.

CHAPTER II

MEMORIES AND MUSINGS

"Now that I have opened that bottle of memories they're pouring out like wine, crimson and bittersweet."

— ELLEN HOPKINS, NOVELIST

23,653

PONDERING my life and existence here on Planet Earth. It is an exercise that can't be done for a large chunk of time because my brain closes down thinking about my own insignificance here on earth. I refuse to take into account the planets, billions of stars and billions of galaxies. I can't fathom those numbers and I can't count that high.

As I write this, 23,653 days is the amount of time I have spent here, on the earthly part of my journey. Those of you who love puzzles or are interested in how old I am, just do the math!! I thought I was old when I counted the years, but boy those individual days sure add up...daily, I've noticed...not much gets by me...

After this deep and intellectual pondering, I have rejected the idea of my own insignificance. I think every single person on this earth makes a difference, each uniquely using their strengths and abilities. A tiny pebble dropped in a pond starts a ripple and changes the pond. I know I am not telling you anything new. This has been said and written many times in various ways. I need to write about it because it is part of my credo that I shared in my first book.

A personal credo defines what you believe and how you live your life. Credo is from Latin and means "I believe." I am going to share it again here because it is meaningful to this writing. It is how I try to live my life...try being the operative word. I am human and I am a work in progress.

Credo

> "I believe in God. I believe no child should go hungry or lack a loving home. I believe that every day on this earth is a gift, another chance to give the world my best self. I believe that we should embrace joy when it is within our reach. I believe if I can touch just one person's life in a positive way, the ripple effect can be a tsunami. I believe

that it is my responsibility to make my little corner of the world better in any way I can. I have faith. I have hope. I have love. I believe."

— LORI LACINA

Take some time to ponder, reflect and examine your own life. Write your own personal credo, celebrate your existence and significance in this world. You matter. Your choices and influence on those in your circle can be life-changing. Ryunosuke Satoro, Japanese writer put it this way: "Individually, we are one drop. Together we are an ocean."

Simple, elegant words. Words to think about. Words to live by. We are not alone, we are the ocean.

MAKING A JOYFUL NOISE

TIP TAP TIP TAP, tip tip tip tap. The speed increases and decreases frequently. I turn to watch the source of the noise, even though I know what it is. A smile crosses my face, as I watch the joyful running steps of very small children. One runs, and the others follow, not so much chasing, but just running for the sheer pleasure of the act. Play at it's best.

Sometimes my inner child longs for the days of carefree running, skipping, jumping, and rolling down hills. No point or purpose except for the rush of adrenaline, the flush on the cheeks and the feeling of pure joy. There is such a small window for childhood and for children to be so free, imaginative and not tethered by the constraints of the structure of life and the demands it can make. When children play, they problem-solve, negotiate, make plans and execute them. They are learning about life in the best possible way. I do fear, in today's world, the childhood window is shrinking, maybe even disappearing. Just my opinion, I think there are too many activities, teams, events, and whatnot that clog up family life and hinder children's ability to imagine, dream, create and play.

When I get the urge to run, jump, and skip, I try to contain myself. No need for any more calls from the neighbors to 911 or to my adult children about my behavior. But in my mind, I am running free, turning somersaults and doing cartwheels. Safer to keep it in my mind these days doesn't hurt as much as if I really pursued these activities. But I will never be too old to sigh for days gone by, and to remember what that absolute freedom felt like.

Encourage the children in your life to go barefoot, climb a tree, make a daisy chain, roll down the hill and run like the wind until they are exhausted! They will be dirty and tired, but their eyes will be sparkling from all their wonderful adventures.

IRONY

THE DEFINITION of irony is to use words/language that means the opposite of the word, usually for humor or emphasis in a remark. So, I am not writing about irony in that way, particularly. I am writing about irony as the opposite of wrinkly. To my way of thinking, if something is wrinkly, you press it, and then it is irony.

I learned about irons and irony from my mom, starting at a young age. When I was a small child, she warned me about the iron she was using, not to touch it as it was very hot. I was a child who demanded proof of things, so I put my entire palm and hand flush against the iron. Yep, Mom was right, it was very hot and I was very burned. No wonder I don't like ironing. Childhood trauma, even if self-inflicted, stays with you! For those who know me, this revelation explains a lot about my personality and misadventures.

It was probably about 6th grade when I was introduced to the act of ironing. I started by ironing handkerchiefs and pillowcases. I was a reluctant student. Why in the world would my mom want me to iron handkerchiefs? I mean, I know what people are going to use those for. And they need to be ironed first? Seriously?? I felt the same way about pillowcases. It wasn't hard work, they were flat, but the logic of why this was necessary eluded me.

My mom had an ironing basket. We didn't have a spray bottle to use, clothes were dampened by sprinkling them with water. I also have a memory of clothes dampened, put in a plastic bag and waiting in the refrigerator to iron.

I was and still to this day am not good at ironing anything that's not flat. Once in a while, I would touch up one of my husband's "no-iron" dress shirts, or a collar on something. There's some irony for you if it is advertised as "no-iron," why am I doing this?

I am living by the Janet Evanovich quote, "When something needs to be ironed I put it in the ironing basket. If a year goes by and the item is still in the basket I throw the item away. This is a good system since eventually, I end up with clothes that don't need ironing."

I feel the same way about items that need to go to the dry cleaners. I try to be careful, but every once in a while, some lovely but nefarious item sneaks through my security system. No matter how much I love the afore-mentioned item, I will hesitate when choosing it to wear if there is another choice. A trip to the dry cleaners is another errand that I don't want to do.

After all this time, and my reluctant ironing, I still have my mom's and grandmother's handkerchiefs. They are a lovely reminder of a nicety of days gone by, pretty and feminine. I am trying to think of a creative way to display them. At my dad's funeral, a dear friend gave me one of her mom's handkerchiefs. I love it and the love that went with the gesture. I carry it with me always.

On your journey today, I wish this for you; clothes that are irony and not wrinkly. If they are wrinkly, go rogue and wear them anyway. There are no wrinkly police that I am aware of, and I know about a lot of different kinds of police. Don't ask, it is a different story!!

MATH AND ROMANCE

I HAVE BEEN BLESSED in my life to have a second chance at love after being widowed. I have written about my very significant gentleman friend in my previous book, as well as here. He is definitely a keeper, and after I relate this story to you, you will be amazed as am I, that he didn't run screaming out the door, and we are still together more than six years later!

We had been dating for five or six weeks. Sometime during this time, I had explained to him that I was watching my caloric intake by counting carbohydrates. As you can imagine, he found this riveting.

For those of you uninitiated in this practice, a carb serving is 15 grams. This information is readily found on the packaging of food and drinks.

One Friday night, we decided to head to the local casino to hear the band in the lounge, have an adult beverage, and maybe even dance a little. My drink of choice was Michelob Ultra beer. I was having a very good time and may have had several... I explained to Verne (aforementioned very significant gentleman friend), that a bottle of Michelob Ultra only has 2 grams of carbs per bottle, which meant I could have seven of said beverage and it would only be one carb serving. At that point, my bottle was empty and being the considerate escort, he asked me if I would like another. I replied in a teasing manner, "Well, have I had 7 yet?" He quickly ordered me another.

I was not inebriated, but rather giddy with the way our relationship was developing, having a good time, and being silly. I can be myself with this man, no dialing it down. He embraces my silliness and outbursts of crazy. He is just the right fit for me. Maybe I was intoxicated, not from the adult beverages, but from the knowledge that I was falling in love again. It is a glorious feeling and I knew that my landing would be safe and memorable.

BELL BOTTOM JEANS

I DON'T MISS much of the clothing trends from my younger days, but bell-bottom jeans were the best. Maybe not so much for the style, although I did rock them back in the day, but because of the time of my life in which they were worn. Purchasing the jeans was an event in itself. We bought our bell-bottom jeans from a newish store called "Garbage." (It was pronounced with an accent on the second syllable, rhymes with mirage.) The jeans were stacked in garbage cans that were turned on their side and in stacks around the store. I also bought my first backpack there, in preparation for beginning classes at the University of Iowa.

I am part of the last population wave that is called the Baby Boomers. This group consists of people born between 1946 and 1964, roughly 76 million people who came of age during the time of the Vietnam War. We are the largest living population of adults. Our group is called the Baby Boomers because we represent a significant increase in births after World War II.

Growing up as a Baby Boomer in a college town let me experience many things. I witnessed many protests against the Vietnam War in downtown Iowa City. Many of the protests were peaceful, but some were not, most downtown businesses experienced broken plate glass windows more than once. I remember one time, there was a group putting themselves between the police and the protesters. Our parents forbade us to go downtown, but...we needed to see what was happening.

We are often called the generation of peace, love, and rock 'n roll, and I am okay with that. In fact, I like it. What is cooler than that?? It was the age of Aquarius, hippies were everywhere and things were groovy.

Tie-dye clothing was popular. We listened to Elvis, the Beatles, the 5th Dimension, Carole King, Ricky Nelson and Hamilton, and Joni Mitchell to name a few. We experienced interesting times, political times, important times, and scary times. So many of our young men were drafted and sent to Vietnam. Not all of them came back.

The times were turbulent. I have always thought that the reason I am still close to many of my high school classmates is because of what we experienced together. We share the same frame of reference for growing up in a very vivid and memorable time in this country's history.

I miss those times in some ways. We were so alive and so engaged in what was happening in our world. The memories I have of coming of age then are good ones. In spite of the turmoil that surrounded us at times, I always felt safe to be myself and safe in my world.

So if you qualify to be a member of this group, find a pair of bell-bottom jeans, put on a psychedelic shirt, add that big peace sign necklace and share your groovy self with the world!

OPEN MY HEART FOR A FRESH START

SITTING HERE in one of my coffee shop offices writing and it is the advent of a new year. Always a time to think of ways to lead a better life, have a fresh start, to make plans and to reflect. New beginnings are everywhere for the taking or making. This year I want to open my heart to these new beginnings and possibilities. I don't want this to be a year like every other year. I want to be in charge, and make things happen...for myself and for others. I want to take on new challenges and recognize opportunities to make the world a little bit better and improve on myself whenever I can.

Zyan Malik, an English singer and songwriter had this to say: "There comes a day when you realize turning the page is the best feeling in the world, because you realize there's so much more to the book than the page you were stuck on." I love this quote. It is difficult to turn the page some-times. You may be stuck on a page, but it is comfortable there and scary to turn to the next one. But turn the page we must, and see what we can write anew.

I feel like a broken record, but I am so passionate about trying.

Try new things. Do something you want to do even if it is a little uncom-fortable for you. Read new books. Meet new people. Have new adven-tures. Bring friends along as you have new experiences. It will be energizing, refreshing and you will feel the satisfaction of a new accom-plishment.

I wish for you to have grace in your heart, peace in your soul, and flowers in your hair. Run like the wind (or in my case, try to walk less slowly!). Drink in the new experiences, pour a little eggnog on your Cheerios and conquer the day!

DUCK, DUCK, GOOSE

OH, the games we played as a child. I have so many happy memories of game-playing with brothers, cousins, and friends. I hope some of these will spark a happy memory of childhood games in your life!!

OUTSIDE GAMES
Freeze Tag
Captain, May I?
Red Light, Green Light
Hopscotch
Foursquare
Duck, Duck, Goose
Kickball
Tether Ball
Secret Agent

INSIDE GAMES
Spoons
War
Ouija Board
Mousetrap
Jacks
Pick Up Sticks
Monopoly
Clue
Mancala
Authors

There are probably many I am forgetting, but these definitely were some favorites. I played a mean game of kickball and foursquare, so bring it on!! Resurrect some of these games for the children in your life, especially the outdoor games. Running and playing outside, regardless of the weather is something kids love. We could play Duck, Duck, Goose for hours in the snow.

"Children need the freedom and time to play. Play is not a luxury. Play is a necessity."

— KAY REDFIELD JAMISON, AMERICAN CLINICAL
PSYCHOLOGIST

I have often and loudly mourned the lack of time for children to play in these crazy times we live in. It hurts my heart when I see children who have no time that is not scheduled or structured with school, sports, and other extracurricular activities.

Don't think I am letting you off the hook, just because you are an adult. If you have to, schedule some time for yourself to play!!

"Your body cannot heal without play. Your mind cannot heal without laughter. Your soul cannot heal without joy."

— CATHERINE RIPPENGER FENWICK, AUTHOR AND
EDUCATOR

So my friends, go forth and play, laugh and be joyful. Find the child within you and set it free!! Find a puddle to stomp in, a rope to jump, or a Duck, Duck, Goose game. It will change your world, and the world around you!

GREETINGS, SALUTATIONS, AND CONDOLENCES

HALLMARK, a business enterprise I admire greatly has served us for many years, providing greeting cards for almost every occasion. Who doesn't love getting a nice card in the mail? However, I have noticed that there are occasions for which greeting cards are not available. Pay attention Hallmark!! Here is my list.

Winning the lottery
Lost pet
Re-marriage
Losing your job
Going to jail
Getting out of jail
Having your identity stolen
Totaling your car
Cosmetic surgery
Bad cosmetic surgery
Re-marrying the person you previously divorced
Losing your driver's license
Outstanding Christmas decorations
Epic fail Christmas decorations
Presidents Day
Mowing your yard
Losing touch with a friend
Your dog bit a bicycle policeman

Maybe I am getting a little too specific, but sometimes you just don't know what to say in a situation. I feel certain Hallmark would be our go-to resource with a little nudging. I like to help out if I can, so here are a couple of possible greeting card verses for unusual situations.

To the friend who totaled their car:

> I heard you totaled your car,
> So glad you weren't at the bar.

Nobody was hurt, all will be fine,
Buy a new car, sign on the line.
If you need a ride, please be aware
Your friends will be glad to drive you everywhere.

To the neighbor:

Dear Neighbor:
Thanks for the mowing of your yard.
This occasion calls for sending you a card.
Heed some friendly advice,
More than once a month would be nice.

Feel free to borrow my simple verses until Hallmark broadens their horizons to include more situational greeting cards. Even better, break out the colored pencils, try some rhyming and create your own greeting cards. As Hallmark would say, "When you care enough to send the very best."

CASTING CALL: THE MOVIE ABOUT MY LIFE

Do you ever think about the casting, logistics, scenery if Hollywood knocked on your door and wanted to make a movie about your life?

Okay, so maybe it's just me. It's not like I spend a great deal of time thinking about this, but it can help pass the time in the dentist's chair, the long line at the Driver's License Station, or during a long and slow base-ball game.

So, who will play the lead, and of course the love interest? Unbeknownst to her, I have chosen Diane Lane to play the part of Lori. There are no well-known actresses that look like me, for obvious reasons; and Lucille Ball is deceased, so I did the best I could. I find Ms. Lane to be quirky, funny, engaging, and a girl next door kind of gal!

Now for the love interest...which would be a lot more fun if I were playing the lead in the story of my life. I have chosen, again, unbeknownst to him, Tom Selleck. A no nonsense man's man, and holy cow, not at all hard to look at. Sam Elliott would be a close second... The roles of my family and friends are not cast, so if you fall into that category, suggestions on whom you would like to see play your part, let me know.

I probably should not wait any longer for Hollywood to find me, the details of my life story are already kind of hazy, so the sooner this happens the better. I don't really know who to call to start the ball rolling. Maybe I could just offer up this opportunity on Facebook and wait for the magic to happen. Surely somebody I know, knows somebody who knows some-body who knows some Hollywood movie magnate's housekeeper…

THIRTY-THREE TREASURES

Mixed, colorful blooms in a ceramic pot

Montage of interesting items on a bookshelf

An ice-cold glass of milk

A very long tree-lined, gravel country road

The waterfall of gingko leaves falling from the tree

Infectious giggling of a toddler

Unexpected visitor

A plump new book by a favorite author

Fluttering of birds at the feeder

Sassy haircut

Crisp two-dollar bill

First sip of coffee

Ritz crackers

New pens

Moonlight through the bedroom window

Re-watching a favorite movie

Soft rain on the roof at night

Sea glass

Orange tulips

Cherry wood

Tree blossoms

Hand-made pottery

Peonies

Spearmint

Acoustic guitar

New baby smell

Warm chocolate chip cookie

Hugs

Book shop cafe

Cartwheels

Cheese popcorn

Midnight blue star-filled sky

Perfect piece of dark chocolate

SUNRISE, SUNSET

"SUNRISE SUNSET," is a song from the Broadway show, "Fiddler on the Roof." The lyrics were written by Sheldon Harnick, an American song-writer, and lyricist. When I typed those words, knowing what I wanted to write about, I had not even thought of this song for a long time. Typing the words had the effect of the tune and lyrics erupting from my memory bank.

I have been thinking about this subject ever since I experienced (not by choice) a milestone birthday this year. How many sunrises do I have left? Of course, I don't know the answer to this, nor does anyone else except the One who paints the stars in the sky. The result of all this thinking (yes, my head hurts!) was to calculate all of the things I have left to do, to see, to experience, to write, and to say.

I am living a heightened appreciation of every day, of every sunrise, of every person in my life. I am not worried about how many sunrises I have left to experience. I do know that I am going to welcome every single one with exuberance and joy.

As the song states, "Sunrise, sunset! Swiftly fly the years, one season following another, laden with happiness and tears." There are sunrises and sunsets every day, and they are free for the taking. I plan to live on the sunrise side of the mountain as long as I can!

The author of one of my favorite books, "Wild," Cheryl Strayed says this: "My mom says there's a sunrise and a sunset every day and you can choose to be there or not. You can put yourself in the way of beauty."

On your personal journey, choose to show up for the beauty.

HEAVY METTLE

MY CONSTANT AND steadfast companion and source for all things "wordy;" Merriam-Webster has been providing authors and normal people definitions and information since 1828. Their definition of the word mettle is as follows: "vigor and strength of spirit or temperament, staying quality: stamina." I love this word and it isn't used nearly enough.

I started thinking about this subject in regards to young adults starting to make their way in the world and specifically their first "real" job. So consider this advice to my grandchildren, nieces and nephews and all other young people in this category.

Entering the world of supporting yourself, paying bills, dealing with the vagaries of the working world is not for the faint of heart. I hope you can find work that you can embrace and be passionate about. Every job is worth doing well and giving it your best effort. Be patient, exceed expectations every day, and your success will know no limits. As far as work, there is no such thing as the perfect job. I have been fortunate to have had a number of wonderful, challenging, rewarding jobs. As much as I loved doing those jobs, there were parts of all those jobs that were tedious and not a walk in the park. You need to get the lemons in order to make the lemonade.

So put your pedal to the mettle, look at each workday as another chance to show your talents and ambition. Push your boundaries-how else will you know what you are capable of? Success often lies just outside our comfort zone. Give the best of yourself to your job, your family, your friends, and your life. Wishing you success, happiness and lemonade days.

MY ADULT BUSY BOARD

JUST RETURNED HOME from a recent road trip to Texas, which involves around 22 hours of quality time in the car with your loved one. This is an immense expanse of time to fill. Regardless of our hours of intellectual and scintillating conversation, one of us may get a wee bit fidgety. Yes, my name is Lori and I struggle to sit still. I don't care to be encaged in small spaces or expected to be relatively still. Granted, the fuel, food, bathroom and the "let me out of the car before I scream" stops do break up the sitting, but it's never enough!!

On the return leg of this journey, I was busily adjusting the climate, the vents, the radio, the navigation system, looking for my iPad, and the usual. I received this look from the driver, you know, that annoyed look men give you when you are touching or moving their things. This was followed by a remark along the lines of, "Are you having fun? Is there anything else you can change?" Well, ladies, it was the tone of the voice that let me know I was being reprimanded...like that has ever stopped me in this lifetime.

I started laughing and said, "Well, this is my adult version of a busy board." Activity or busy boards for children have zippers, buttons, grabby things, pockets, things to pull on, hit, wind...well you get the idea. It had never occurred to me before, but the fancy consoles in today's automobiles do have a variety of things to keep one entertained. Add that to my iPhone, iPad, notecards (to jot down story ideas), my personal calendar and the 248 other items in my "purse," and I can usually manage to stay occupied.

After all of those things lose their luster, we turn to the audiobook. We like some of the same kinds of books, so I usually have a selection downloaded for us to listen to. It does help break up a long day on the road. This trip we listened to "The Ex-Wife," billed as a psychological thriller. It did have a lot of twists and turns. I was slightly annoyed by the *then* and *now* chapters, present to flashback throughout the entire book. It worked well enough for this book, but I am a "just tell me the story from start to finish" kind of girl!! If you haven't tried listening to books on road trips, I highly recommend it.

Make a list, prepare for that next road trip and hit the road. Don't forget to pack your entertainment, familiarize yourself with the Busy Board in the car in which you will be traveling, and look forward to an enjoyable voyage.

Izaac Walton said, "Good company in a journey makes the way seem shorter." Very true, but I'm still packing the entertainment…

SWEET SOUNDS OF LIFE

WOODEN SCREEN DOOR slamming into the door frame

Crackling, hissing, popping of the wood fire

Last notes of a haunting melody

Soft, gentle rainfall during the night

Wind chimes

The whispering sweetness of a secret

Ocean waves crashing on the beach

A song that sounds like a memory

Scatter, clatter, and cacophony of a family holiday

The soft silence of snowfall

A child's first words

Chirping, chattering birds at dawn

Sounds of summer drifting through the open window

Bells

A train whistle in the distance at midnight

Bubbling, simmering stew

Thunder

Giggles of gaggles of toddlers

The rhythmic repetition of the porch swing moving to and fro

All-encompassing sound of complete silence

The sounds of life

William Shakespeare said, "The earth has music for those who listen."

Actively listen today and absorb the sweetness of the music of your life. It surrounds you and will astound you with its melody if you take the time to listen not only with your ears, but with your heart.

"TINIKLE" MY FANCY

I HAVE BEEN TAKING lots of trips down Memory Lane lately. It is a great place to visit. The parking is free and the sights are beautiful. It encompasses all the places you've ever been, all the people you've ever known, and maybe most importantly, every age you have ever been. Some friends and I were wistfully reminiscing about childhood antics, and a particular memory popped into my mind. I loved a game called tinikling.

At least three players were needed, and it involved two poles, usually bamboo, that two of the players held, one on each end of the poles, slapping the floor and then the poles together in different rhythms. The third player executed a series of dance/skip steps between, over and outside the poles. A second dancer could also be added to the fun.

I recently learned this was originally a Philippine folk dance. I am pretty sure we learned it in gym class in junior high as a unit, and it became popular with kids outside of school. Good exercise and you have to be nimble and have some rhythm to not get your ankles smacked by the poles! Not only did that smart like crazy, it meant your turn to be the dancer was over. Nobody wanted to walk around with bruised ankles, which was proof you weren't a good tinikler!! Good thing there was no social media to broadcast that, just the playground chatter!

Another similar game was Chinese Jump Rope. We could make our own, by stringing a huge number of stronger rubber bands together, until you have a very big circle. The game was played similarly to tinikling. Two people with their feet inside the ends of the jump rope, stretch the rubber bands out into an oblong. One or more dancers or jumpers, chanting jump rope chants. Most of these games were played by girls, and many of the rhymes and chants involved kissing a boy, love and marriage; a definite pattern.

Here are several of the chants I remember from jumping rope and Chinese Jump Rope. Just saying them to myself, brings a picture to my mind of a group of girls at recess on the cement area on the side of Longfellow school, jumping rope.

Cinderella, dressed in yellow
Went upstairs to kiss her fellow
Made a mistake and kissed a snake
How many doctors did it take? 1,2,3...counting jumps till jumper missed

Ice cream soda
Lemonade punch
Tell me the name
Of my honey-bunch...A, B, C, ...again until the jumper missed and the
letter she missed on would be the clue to her beau's name.

Carefree days, fresh air, play that contained exercise, cooperation and socializing with friends...hard to beat. I don't know if children still play these kinds of games at recess or after school. I hope so. Life was simpler then. Extracurricular activities at that age were Girl or Boy Scouts, 4-H, music lessons and church activities. It left plenty of time for creative, unstructured freedom to play and explore. A very important part of a child's development and happiness.

Fred Rogers, TV personality said, "Play is often talked about as if it were a relief from serious learning. But for children, play is serious learning. Play is really the work of childhood."

Remember the days you played as a child. Incorporate some play and some joy into every day. Jump on the swingset, roll in the grass, lay on a blanket and cloud watch. Play will refresh you and heal your soul.

TWINKLE LIGHTS AND CHEESE PIZZA

IT WAS A DAY TO REMEMBER, to mark on the calendar, to wallow in the glory of it all...a day spent at home, with an enormous "To Do" list and the will to survive and thrive. I often create these daunting lists for myself and rarely complete all the tasks...not because there is not enough time, but because I don't want to. Just like the toddler who doesn't want to take a nap, some days I just refuse to do things I don't like to do.

I don't know what was different about this day, maybe it was the background music I was playing, maybe it was something magic in the air, maybe I had too much coffee. I was rocking and rolling all day, checking my list, crossing things off. I also did chores that weren't on the list and crossed those off. I was unstoppable. I won't pretend I was Wonder Woman, but it is true that no one has ever seen us together...

I spent the ENTIRE day, which in my view ends at 4:30 p.m. or so. One must not tarnish the happy hour time with chores. I completed everything on my list..repeat...I completed EVERYTHING on my list.

I don't think that has ever happened before. I was happy, feeling accomplished and tired. I was as happy as a chunky baby with a handful of mac and cheese. To reward myself, I decided to order a small cheese pizza for dinner and turned on the white lights on my deck. These are used year-round, and despite what some people call them, they are not Christmas lights. They are party lights.

Sigh...what a day...a cheese pizza and twinkle lights kind of day. It is indeed the little things that can make one happy. My wish for you is to embrace the little things that make you happy, celebrate large and small accomplishments, and don't forget the twinkle lights.

THE ARTIST'S CANVAS

As I WATCH the early morning sky, the sun rising in the east, I survey my supplies, choose my brushes, and examine the canvas closely. Where shall I begin? Translating the Master's work in my own way is a challenging task; one that I can't always manage the way I see it.

One must begin somewhere, and so I shall. I begin the arduous task of applying makeup to my morning face...I plan to go out into the world today, and not wanting to scare small children or create a scene, I will attempt to repair, cover, and hide the ravages of time. It is a reflective time, as I study the changes that time and tide have wrought on my face. I realize that there is just so much that foundation and concealer can cover. One must not expect the impossible!!

I do the best I can to cover the dark circles, the imperfections and the wrinkles. I yearn for the days when a whisk of blush, some mascara and a swipe of lip gloss would be enough to send me out the door. Ahhh, the gifts of youth that I didn't appreciate as much as I should have at the time. It was all part of those carefree days, where summer was endless, we were immortal and life was a flurry of activity.

A couple of years ago, I had a detached retina. During the exam, the doctor noted there was a cataract near the retinal tear, so they would fix that as well. Great results (torturous recovery), almost perfect eyesight in the left eye. The next year's eye exam detected I had a cataract in the other eye and that would need to be fixed. Again, good results, except...tests seemed to indicate I would not need to wear glasses all the time. Are you kidding me?? The glasses nicely cover possible dark circles under my eyes and create a distraction from my face.

Much to my relief, I do need a very small correction. I really just need them to read, but a tiny distance correction does help, not only my eyes but my face. Whew!! What a relief!! I really do sort of, kind of need glasses. The added bonus is that I have several pairs and change them out depending on my outfit, my mood, and the weather!! Another fun thing about glasses is using them as a prop. You can take them off dramatically at appropriate moments.

This somewhat tongue in cheek reflection also reminds me that I have earned every wrinkle, laugh line, age spot, sun damage and year that shows on my face. I am still able to dream dreams, to work to make them come true and to not only cherish the memories of the past but work diligently to create new memories every day. I can learn new things, marvel at the world around me, stay up as late as I care to, skip making the bed, and have dessert for breakfast if the mood strikes me!! Life as an "older" adult kind of rocks in some ways!!

Fashion designer, Diane Von Furstenberg said, "My face reflects the wind and sun and dust from the trips I've taken. My face carries all my memories. Why should I erase them?" To that, I say "Brava," Ms. Von Furstenberg. Thanks for putting into words so succinctly how we should feel about aging.

Embrace your age, whatever it may be. Count the wrinkles as if they were merit badges. Reminisce about the happy memories that created all those laugh lines. Greet the world every day with happy anticipation, and the canvas you present to the world will be a masterpiece.

THE APPLE A DAY MYTH

I LOVE CRISP CRUNCHY APPLES. Honeycrisp, September Song, Pink Lady, Gala, Fuji, love them all. The sweet deliciousness, the satisfying crunch, and of course, the virtuous smug feeling that I am eating a healthy snack. This is a long-held belief of mine for as long as I can remember. I would eat an apple every single day. Every single day. Sometimes two. Hold the presses, I am calling for a recount! I have been misled by produce growers, health professionals, and society in general.

I am at this very moment, waiting for my appointment with a University of Iowa dietician, who will undoubtedly change my life. After some delightful hydrogen breath testing to see if I have a food intolerance that is making me ill, the answer was yes. I can't tolerate fructose, my system won't process it. I have done some minimal research and am hoping the dietician will help me navigate the fructose information highway.

Fructose is in almost everything. Using fruit as an example, some fruits are better than others. Apples are not one of those fruits. They are the worst. I may no longer have an apple every day, or even forever. In what universe is this fair?? I am not really exaggerating, I am quoting the dietician. I suppose I could have a small one once in a while. I am bereft. A life without apples...and other fruits. Instead of my apple a day, I am now encouraged to have a Vitamin C supplement every day to replace the fruits I may no longer have. Trust me, it is not a worthy substitute.

Can I get a second opinion? Is there such a thing as a fructologist?

Adding insult to injury, three different health professionals have now said to me that a limited fructose diet is very hard. Thanks for the support. Do you know me? If you tell me something is hard, I will rock it. Is it harder than having surgery, radiation and chemo for cancer? I don't think so. Life is full of very hard things. My food deprivation is a minor inconvenience. I am not happy about it, but it could have been many things that are much worse making me ill.

I learned about this three days before we left for a week-long vacation in

Boston. Great… However, I can have seafood, butter, and french fries. I will survive!! It has created some interesting interactions between me and wait-staff all over Boston and surrounding areas.

We stopped for lunch at a local restaurant in Concord. There was a panini sandwich on the menu that looked really good, and I liked the sides that came with it. Bread, however, can be a problem. I am a problem solver, so I asked to have that menu item without the bread. The server started to write down my order and then stopped. She said, "You want a panini without the bread?" I answered in the affirmative. She looked at me as if I lost my mind. I recognize the look as I get it often. She rolled her eyes so hard, I think she saw her brain. She stood there for a minute, shook her head and walked away.

We chuckled to ourselves, wondering what I would actually get when our food was served. It came and it was perfect. The entree was grilled meat-loaf topped with mozzarella cheese. I received a perfectly "smashed" piece of meatloaf. A panini without the bread. How hard was that? Let's think outside the box people!!

So, now it begins. A lifetime routine of watching what is in the food I eat. I choose to think about the foods I can eat, rather than the foods I can't. Other than those darn apples. I have been apple free for 13 days now. I wonder if there is a support group. I will continue to navigate this nutritional maze and change the way I think about food. I will start to eat to live, rather than live to eat.

I can do hard things. I have done hard things. Life has tested me and I think I have passed the test. You can do hard things. You have done hard things. Whatever is challenging you in your life right now, figure it out. Work on the things you can control, and learn to deal with the things you can't control. William J. Brenner, Jr., Former Associate Justice of the U.S. Supreme Court said this, "We must meet the challenge rather than wish it were not before us."

Go forth, meet your challenges, gather your tribe, do your best every day and pray for strength from the Creator of the Universe and The Keeper of the Stars. He walks beside you on your journey through life and grants you courage, strength, peace, and mercy.

BROWN SUEDE SHOES

MANY OF YOU reading the title will think I am dazed and confused since I am an Elvis fan. I promise you, I do know that Elvis sang about blue suede shoes, not brown. Someday I am going to own a pair of blue suede shoes, but I digress...Brown suede shoes are the topic of this story!

I was a sophomore or junior in high school. A friend who was in one of my classes, I can't even remember which one, but I can remember where we sat in the classroom!! She always had the "coolest" clothes, so I always observed and took notes about her outfits. At some point, she acquired a pair of shoes that I coveted. They were brown suede, high chunky heels, and they tied. I thought they were so sophisticated and admired them every day she wore them.

Sometimes dreams do come true, and I was able to buy an identical pair of those shoes with my Hy-Vee paycheck. Just putting them on made me feel like a different girl. I would sit in my room at home, trying them on with my pajamas, or shorts, or whatever I had on at the moment, so I could admire them on my feet.

I got so much enjoyment out of those shoes. I have a picture of them somewhere because I wore them to the Homecoming dance. Homecoming dances were not the crazy, splashy dress kind of affairs when I was in high school. Many girls wore wool skirts and sweaters. I paired my fancy shoes with a dark pink dress. It was very short (yes, it was the mini-skirt era), buttoned up the front and I think it had a white or cream collar. I can see it yet today in my mind. I weighed about 100 pounds then, so my long skinny legs were on full display. I was very fashionable!!

The really interesting thing about those shoes is that they are back in fashion!! I saw a very similar pair while browsing through the shoe department recently. As I often think when I observe current fashion trends, there is really nothing new. Fashions come in and out of style. Everything is a recycled version of something in the past.

I know you are all wondering if I bought the look-a-like shoes that have happy memories for me. I was tempted, but have not yet succumbed! I need another pair of shoes like Barnes and Noble needs more books. I like to think of it more as a collection of shoes. It sounds so much better. After all, people collect art, cars, and antiques, why not shoes?

It's not that I want more shoes, but they keep making them in my size. I feel compelled to rescue them and provide a forever home for them.

Shoes are so important, people sing songs about them…

"Blue Suede Shoes" Elvis Presley
"These Boots Are Made for Walking" Nancy Sinatra
"Whose Bed Have Your Boots Been Under?" Shania Twain
"Red High Heels" Kellie Pickler
"Boogie Shoes" KC and the Sunshine Band
"The Christmas Shoes" NewSong

As many great people have advised before me, life is short: eat the cake, take the trip and buy the shoes. Especially buy the shoes!!

MUST DO LIST

Think with my heart.
Take a deep breath now and again.
Care for others.
Be thankful.
Take care of myself.
Value the talents of others.
Encourage someone.
Remember the value of time and what I choose to spend it on.
Send a note to a friend.
Have fun.
Make a difference for one person.
Write down my thoughts.
Share.
Take a walk.
Appreciate the beauty of the world around me.

SOMETIMES I NEED to remind myself, what is important in my life, what I should be spending my time doing, and why am I here? Life is full of obstacles, twists, turns, and the unexpected. It is very easy to be distracted and stray from the path we want to be traveling. Anita Krizzan (author) said, "You don't have to move mountains. Simply fall in love with life. Be a tornado of happiness, gratitude, and acceptance. You will change the world just by being a warm, kind-hearted human being."

Fall in love with life every day, over and over. You will never be disappointed, and you will change your life and the lives around you.

EVOLUTION OF STYLE

THE DEFINITION of evolution is the gradual transformation of an object, usually from simple to more complex. However, I have noticed that sometimes, the evolution is not in the change of the object, but in the change of the name. I am thinking of a particular garment that I wore as a young girl in elementary school. We called them pedal pushers.

In the Northeastern part of the country, they were and may still be called clam diggers. These two names have a direct correlation to an activity, in which you would not like to wear full-length pants, bicycling and, wait for it...digging for clams. Love it when description equals functionality.

Funny thing, I still wear those garments today. No, I can't fit into my pedal pushers from days gone by. I know, surprising, but that's life. I did rock those things in the 5th grade, however! What's old is new again, and now I wear capris or crops, which are basically the same thing as pedal pushers. I think pedal pushers sound like an adventure waiting to happen. Capris sound like a juice drink that toddlers are given. Crops are what we grow in the Heartland.

There are so many fashion trends that get their time in the sun, fade away, and then years later come blazing back. Examples from my lifetime: paisley, culottes, fringed boots/moccasins, and mini-skirts to name a few. All of these were popular at some time in my life, junior high to college...and they have all come back and been "discovered" by a younger generation. It makes me laugh, sometimes makes me cry when an unattractive fad rears its ugly head again!

French fashion designer, Coco Chanel said it best, "Fashion comes and goes but style lasts forever." Find your style, and rock it!! Classic and elegant are two fashions that never go out of style!!

CHECK ENGINE LIGHT

AGING, which is a nice way of saying "getting old" is not a bad thing. Every birthday I celebrate I am grateful to have. I am still here on this earthly journey, enjoying my life, my loved ones, my friends. God isn't done with me here.

I know you are now anticipating the dreaded "but." So here it comes. I have earned every day, every wrinkle, every ache and pain and every tiny bit of wisdom I have gained in the roughly 24,000 days I have survived. 60 may be the new 40, but 9:00 is the new midnight. 70 isn't old if you are a tree.

The last few years have tested me. Detached retina, cataract surgery, cracked ribs, nerve damage, and fructose intolerance are the latest additions to my resume. My mind is as quick as it ever was (in my opinion). I still have the equivalent of 47 web browsers open at any given moment and will randomly switch conversational subjects without warning. My girlfriends totally can follow these seemingly unconnected thoughts. It seems to be a female attribute.

I still schedule myself into crazy amounts of activities sometimes, but I have now learned how to hit the switch for my energy-saving mode. Naps are a wonderful thing, and I give myself permission to have one anytime the mood strikes. Laundry can wait. Emptying the dishwasher can wait. Dust will not kill you. Taking a much-needed break can heal your body and soul.

My check engine light might go on every now and then, and I am perplexed by gravity on a regular basis, but I am here and grateful for every day. A Swedish proverb advises this: "Those who wish to sing...always find a song." Find your song and sing it loudly and proudly and the world will sing along.

GEORGIE PORGIE

I HAVE VERY fond memories of my school days at Longfellow Elementary School on Seymour Avenue, in Iowa City. I loved school, couldn't wait to start Kindergarten, and my love of these places of learning followed me throughout my school days. (I secretly still like taking a class and having homework. Don't tell anyone, it is one of my guilty pleasures.) I made many friends there, many of whom are still in my life. I am thankful for the days there, and the special people who populated my K-6 life!!

Elementary school is about more than reading, 'riting and 'rithmetic as the old rhyme goes. It is about making friends, learning how to interact with groups and individuals, negotiation, and recess!!

An interaction that I had in the third grade, could have scarred me for life, but being the survivor that I am, I have put it behind me and moved on with my life. Although, maybe the fact that I am writing about it, tells me I have moved on, but not forgotten.

It was recess time and the normal laughing and frolicking on the playground ensued. Boys often liked to chase the girls, which caused us to shriek with fear and delight. We never learned that if you don't run they can't chase you, and if they caught us, they had no idea what to do with us...until the incident. This particular day, I was being chased by a classmate, whose name I still remember, Joey Briggs. Joey, if you are out there, bless your heart!! Joey chased me, caught me, and then horror of horrors, kissed me on the cheek. I returned to class sobbing, telling the teacher about this traumatic event and hoping to get Joey "in trouble." What else would be the point of our tattling in those days?? I don't remember if Joey got in trouble, probably not as it wasn't a felony...

Thinking about those days reminded me of a childhood poem that I loved. The origins of this ditty is an English language nursery rhyme that may have been around since the late 1800s. So here it is:

"Georgie Porgie, pudding and pie,
Kissed the girls and made them cry.

> When the boys came out to play
> Georgie Porgie ran away."

I guess the Georgies and Joeys of the world have been chasing and kissing girls for a lot of years!! I smile fondly, remembering that world of rhymes, innocence, recess and reading "Dick and Jane" books. Maybe this will spark a memory of yours, from back in the day, when life was simpler, choices more limited and the playground beckoned.

Take a page from your past, relive the moments, try to remember every small detail, and enjoy. Share these great stories with your family, they will love it!

WHAT DO THE LYRICS REALLY MEAN?

"MACARTHUR PARK," an iconic song written by Jimmy Webb and released in 1968. Therefore, like many of you of a certain age, I have been listening to this song for decades...not necessarily on purpose.

It was a very popular song and still turns up quite a bit on Sirius radio.

A mournful, evocative, wrenching song. I sang along with it solemnly with my friends in high school. I did not know then, and still, am not sure now what some of the lyrics mean. So I decided to take a closer look at it.

The songwriter is telling a story about MacArthur Park, which is a real place. Somewhat lyrical words about what he is seeing. The most confusing lyrics, to me, in a what the heck, kind of way are as follows:

"Someone left the cake out in the rain
I don't think that I can take it
'Cause it took so long to bake it
And I'll never have that recipe again.
Oh no."

As a younger person, I never really cared what that meant, I just belted it out with my friends like we knew what we were doing. As I have continued to hear this song, the whole cake thing started to intrigue me. As a fan of many music genres, but country music in particular which is often very literal, I had to wonder...Did someone bake the guy a birthday cake, and leave it out in the rain? Was it on purpose? So I decided to look into the matter a little further. Investigative reporting, right here!!

According to the different stories I read, the songwriter was writing about things he saw at this park, including a cake that was left out in the rain. It is a song about a love affair that played out in the park in some manner. As I reread the lyrics, it reminds me of stream of consciousness writing, where you just write, letting your emotions and feelings fill the page without regard to proper structure, punctuation, or any other convention. The emotions certainly shine through in this song. Probably why it was a great song for angst-filled teen-age girls looking for acceptance, love and their place in life. It tells a story, but one that you have to examine closely and read between the lines to furrow out the meaning.

The more I think about "MacArthur Park," I want to write a story like that. Beware, my readers, you may be subjected to a stream of consciousness, what does she mean, is she crazy, kind of story in this book...we will see.

> "A painter paints pictures on canvas. But musicians paint their picture on silence."

> — LEOPOLD STOWKOWSKI, AN ENGLISH CONDUCTOR OF
> POLISH DESCENT.

This quote is so profound, it made my heart ache a little...in a good way!

Wishing you music that pleases your ears, touches your heart and gives you an appreciation for the talented songwriters that can paint a picture on silence.

DATING OVER 40 OR 50 OR ???

It seems necessary to me, to start this with a very well-known quote, as I have not read anything else that seems as apropos. "What's in a name? That which we call a rose by any other name would smell as sweet." William Shakespeare

This is not a story about roses or Shakespeare. It is partly about names or labels for people when you are dating over the age of 40. (Well, maybe WAY over the age of 40) The primary question that comes up is how to "label" the man I am in a relationship with/dating. After six years, are we still dating? What are we doing? (I am sure he asks himself this frequently when I get one of my crazy ideas or have a misadventure.) But, I digress...

Labeling comes up when I introduce him to people. I suppose I could just announce his name and leave it at that. I don't like the feel of that. He is so important in my life. I can't say, my husband, or fiance, which defines a relationship quickly and concisely. He says he is my "main squeeze," and my "most significant other."

Other labels I have used/heard:

- Life partner-As opposed to my tennis partner??
- Better half-Of what?
- Other half-I don't even know what this means!!
- Beau-When I hear this, I am wondering why this gentleman isn't looking for Scarlett at the plantation.
- Gentleman caller-This could be a telemarketer
- Soulmate-Too much and not enough!
- Boyfriend...really?? At this age of life, if you truly have a "boyfriend," time to raise the bar and find a grown-up man!
- Significant other-isn't everybody?

I really couldn't resist this somewhat serious, somewhat tongue-in-cheek discourse about what to call the special man in my life. I don't think he really cares what I call him, as long as I keep calling!!

In the larger scheme, labels are for cans, jars and filing cabinets, not people!! W.C. Fields said, "It ain't what they call you, it's what you answer to." Labels limit people and make them smaller than they are. I am a sister, grandmother, aunt, stepmother, educator, quilter, and author, to name a few things. I am much more than any one of those things, and all of those things combined. You, too, are more than any label given to you. A label can never define the uniqueness that makes you who you are.

On your journey, embrace the imperfect perfectness that makes you the unique person given to the world by the One who paints the skies and hangs the stars.

SOLITUDE

SOLITUDE...I feel relaxed, floating through the day as if on a raft on the quiet river. It has been quite some time since I have had a day all to myself. No places to be, no obligations. Nobody, nowhere, nohow. It was a couple of hours after I rose from a wonderful night's sleep that I realized how content I was. Me, myself, and I as we used to say as children.

I must confess, the lack of solitude is my own fault. I am pretty social and like to be with others. I am also a part-time guest teacher, but sometimes I find it hard to say no when asked to fill a position for the day. Today, I am remembering why I need to say no sometimes.

Solitude gives me time to think without all the noise of the outside world. I have given myself permission to sit and do nothing but look outside or at my feet on the coffee table. It is doubly satisfying when the outside world is having a cold and gloomy day, while I nestle into my cozy home.

Puttering is also a component of solitude. I wander around the house, rearranging this, moving that. I find myself in my quilting studio working for a bit on a project that is waiting there. Into the kitchen to stir the aromatic pot of chili that is cooking, adding a little of this and a little of that. Time to organize the pile of papers, put things away, satisfaction in the completion of small tasks. I am very good at puttering. As a new acquaintance said to me, "It's not bragging if you can do it." Puttering allows me to glide through the rooms, being distracted before I get to my destination. It satisfies my need to have eighty-seven projects in different states of completion.

Solitude, wandering, puttering are good for the soul. I have time to think, plan, dream, and nap. Yes, I said nap, it is an essential component to this day. Solitude refreshes my creativity, improves my outlook, and gives me perspective about my thoughts.

The world can be a noisy place, interfering with your mind and body's ability to be in alignment and perfect balance. A dose of solitude, at least for me is just what the doctor ordered.

"Solitude is the soul's holiday, an opportunity to stop doing for others and to surprise and delight ourselves instead."

— KATRINA KENISON, AUTHOR

Have yourself a celebration of solitude, so you are able to give your best self to the world.

TIME TRAVEL AND STRAWBERRY ICE CREAM

I MAY HAVE HAD a "Wrinkle in Time" moment last night. It was about 8:30 and I was quasi-watching the University of Houston vs. SMU football game. This phenomenon occurred because my gentleman friend had been watching the game, left to go home and the television remained on that channel...as it does when the remote is not used to change it. I was simultaneously doing little tasks around my home. I was in my quilting studio which needed a great deal of attention. Words can't describe the sight in that room. I have a lot of words, but not enough for that hot mess. I was busily making progress and setting it to rights.

This is where the tesseract happened. In the "Wrinkle in Time," which is a favorite young adult book; time is the fourth dimension and the fifth dimension (for people of a certain age..no it is not the "Age of Aquarius singing group!) is the tesseract which is a portal through time and space. Translation: time travel!

One minute I am working on the self-inflicted mess in my quilting room, and the next minute, I am eating vanilla ice cream with strawberries on top, sitting on the couch watching a Hallmark Christmas movie. There was no segue, no transitional moment, no planning or preparation, it just happened. The secondary amazing part of all this is that the strawberries needed to be cleaned and cut up. So I used a knife, a sharp object without prior planning. Not necessarily something I am proficient at doing. I have references and testimonials, thankfully no video.

I am relishing the ice cream treat and enjoying the movie. Hallmark movies are predictable and I am okay with that. It is comforting to watch a story, knowing despite the angst and drama, it will all work out in the end.

Life has proven to me over and over again, that things do not always work out in the end. Happy endings are not promised and dreams do not always come true. Fortunately, the indefatigable human spirit always has hope. We get up every day, do what needs to be done, and have the belief that things can and will get better.

This quote from an unknown source describes it perfectly; "Hope is the ability to hear the melody of the future. Faith is the courage to dance to it."

Therefore, dear readers, wake up every morning, listen to the music and have the courage to dance. From personal experience, a little ice cream and strawberries might help as well.

WHERE IS THE HOT WATER?

NOTHING like bountiful hot water on a cold winter day when you shower. My hot water source seems plentiful and strong. I can run the dishwasher or the washing machine, and both showers can be in use and there is no lack of hot water. However...there is a hot water mystery at my house, at least it is a mystery to me. To be honest, many things are a mystery to me.

Daily, I turn on the shower and there is hot water in mere seconds. Hot water, no waiting. Twelve feet away, and I measured spigot to spigot, resides one of my bathroom sinks. When I turn on the water there, minutes pass before the water is even passably warm, let alone hot. Am I wrong? Is this a mystery? The sinks are not on an outside wall, they are nicely protected and insulated. So, where is the hot water?

I haven't needed a plumber, so I have had no opportunity to casually ask that question. My dad who was a master of all trades, including being a pipefitter probably could have answered the question if I had thought to ask him before he died. I do not want to call a plumber and ask the question, I get enough strange looks/responses from service people as it is. I am pretty sure my picture is on the bulletin board in the employee break area at Menards. Why else would they all disappear when I am seeking assistance? I always know exactly what I need, I may not know the name of it, but I can describe it...you know that black squiggly doo-hickey that connects that straight thing to the other squiggly thing. Alas, so many mysteries I can't solve!! But I am thankful for my plumbing. James P. Gorman (Chairman and CEO of Morgan Stanley) said, "If you consider the contribution of plumbing to human life, the other sciences fade into insignificance." I guess if this big shot can ponder about plumbing, my questions are also relevant!!

THE OLD IS NEW AGAIN

IT IS SO much fun when objects or fashion from "back in the day," make a triumphant return. The best part is watching the younger crowd become all excited about this trendy new thing that they have to have. Yep, kids, been there, bought that, used it up and threw it away.

The latest old but new shiny object to waltz onto the retail stage is the Polaroid Camera. There are other brands of this camera, but I am referring to Polaroid as the camera from the past. What a miraculous thing!! Take a picture and watch it develop before your very eyes, and a hard copy to keep! In spite of all the "instant" pictures we take today with our phones and tablets, this icon from the past has made a comeback. It is available in fun trendy colors to choose from. I love that many of the young people in my life have embraced this camera and are having fun with it.

When we take pictures with our phones, it is easy to take a dozen or more of one scene, person or event to ensure we get a "good" one. If you only have a Polaroid camera with you, and enough film for twenty pictures, it seems that we would be more selective with our choices of shots. Instead of clicking away, maybe we stop and enjoy the moment and take a bit more time to take the picture. Just a thought.

A quote from an unknown source sums it up perfectly for me: "We take photos as a return ticket to a moment otherwise gone." Yes, indeed. We want those photos to capture a special moment, so we can relive it over and over again. We can share it with family and friends. We own that moment in time. Take the pictures with whatever kind of camera works for you, but don't get so caught up in taking the shot, that you don't have time to truly relish the moment, and capture the emotions, not just the picture.

IS THERE EVER TOO MUCH SUGAR AT EASTER?

I AM certain many parents and dentists would agree there is too much sugary candy at Easter. I, however, have taken too much sugar to a whole new level. I don't like to brag, but when I do something, I like to go all in.

Easter Sunday morning, post breakfast, pre-church. I am busily doing some tidying up in the kitchen. I made carrot cake on Saturday for our Easter dinner, and not everything was put away. So, wanting everything to be neat and clean when I start preparing Easter dinner a/k/a trashing my kitchen again, I am scurrying around. The last item to get placed in the pantry is the sugar canister. I washed it after emptying it on Saturday, so it is clean, full of sugar and ready to be tucked away. I lift it up to the highest shelf in the pantry and as I lift it, the lid catches and pops off, and sugar starts to go everywhere for what seems like hours before I can right the canister and put it down. I may have had a sugar rush.

I wanted to cry, but there was nothing to do but start cleaning up the mess. Did I mention that the pantry shelving is the wire type, so the sugar, thanks to gravity, my arch nemesis, proceeds to cover all the can goods and supplies in the pantry? Hazmat teams don't work on Easter Sunday, so there is nothing to be done, but to empty the pantry and begin de-sugaring. Sugar is a stealthy, insidious substance to deal with. After wiping down every can, box, etc, I began the big job. I swept. I vacuumed and mopped, vacuumed and mopped. I could still feel the grittiness underfoot on the kitchen floor. So I repeated the cleaning steps. This fun activity started before church and had to be finished after church.

The bright side of this sugar fiasco is that my pantry got re-organized, alphabetized, categorized and looks fantastic. That aspect is more satisfying now than when I was working on it!

The moral of the story is that too much sugar, indeed, can be hazardous to your mental and physical well-being. Particularly when gravity decides to get involved. As they say, all's well that ends well...or do these types of things happen in threes? I wondered that this morning before I left for the coffee shop to do some writing. My question may have been answered when I broke a Christmas wine glass. Don't even ask why I would have been in the position to break a wine glass at 8:00 a.m. Some things are better left alone.

Mark Zuckerberg, CEO of Facebook, said it well, "Move fast and break things. Unless you are breaking stuff, you are not moving fast enough."

I am with you Mr. Zuckerberg, it seems I am moving fast enough!

SKILLS I NEED TO ACQUIRE

As you read my list, I am sure some of the items will catch your attention, and you will think, she COULD do that if she tried. Sometimes my lack of time and my unwillingness to devote the necessary time to a project get in the way of my being able to accomplish it!! Surprise, surprise!!

- Cartwheels
- Sing well and with confidence
- Have a natural gracefulness
- Somersaults
- Speak a second language fluently
- Own a local book shop
- Have a room as a dedicated library/office
- Minimize my wardrobe
- Waltz
- Cartwheels (I know, again)
- Cook with creativity and abandon
- Finish my second book (if you are reading this, I did it!)
- Publish a story in a magazine
- Keep better records
- Learn to pack for traveling
- Do not bring everything I own on a trip (see above)
- Cartwheels
- Write a bestselling book

I probably should explain the cartwheels obsession!! It just seems to me the ultimate way to celebrate an accomplishment, be spontaneous, express your joy, surprise passers-by and feel like a kid again!! If I could find someone teaching cartwheel lessons for the young at heart, I would be all over that.

Make your own list of projects you want to accomplish, things you dream of doing or trying. I would bet that you could check some of those things off if you focus!! Today is the best day to start. Later, next week, tomorrow, when I have time, are idea killers. Do something today to start the realization of a dream!!

Henry David Thoreau who was an American essayist, poet, historian, naturalist, abolitionist, just to name a few of his accomplishments, said, "What you get by achieving your goals is not as important as what you become by achieving your goals."

Spend some time dreaming some dreams, setting some goals, and start treating the world to the best version of yourself. It will change your life and the lives of those you touch.

NOT A CREATURE WAS STIRRING ...

THERE IS nothing more lonely than being awake in the still of the night. Tired, but unable to sleep, the night taunts me. It is so very quiet, yet I hear every whisper of the wind, every creak of the house, every sound outside in the inky black night. This is a familiar place to me, I come here more often than I would like, but the relative stillness doesn't calm me.

Why, I ask? Why won't my mind slow down and let me drift into the restful comfort of sleep? My eyes are tired and my body wants to rest. Yet, here I roam the dark rooms of my house, looking for a remedy to my wakefulness. There are no overwhelming or pressing concerns that I am worrying about. Thoughts scatter through my mind like autumn leaves on a windy night.

Home remedies, such as a warm glass of milk do not appeal to me. I gag thinking about drinking warm milk. I like mine in a glass with ice in it.

People think I am strange (well there's another story for you) but why do you think they call it "ice-cold" milk? I rest my case. I like a cup of tea now and then, but making one in the middle of the night seems like too much work, and not sure it would work anyway. I am considering a new approach: something room temperature, warm, amber in color, easy to procure and prepare. Brandy, yes, I am thinking about brandy to warm my soul and slow my brain. I rarely drink anymore, but this deserves some consideration.

I do have to admit, I have never used my nighttime wandering to slide into a session at my laptop to write about this experience. However, tonight this is happening, and I am writing. My eyes are starting to droop a little more, this might be the answer I have been seeking!

As a child and up through my early twenties, I suffered from somnambulism...I was a sleepwalker. In those days of yore, parents didn't seek help for their child. They would just put me back to bed. Their first clue that I was experiencing this problem was the fact that I fell out of the top bunk of the bed several nights in a row. I was trying to go for a walk. Fortunately, I incurred no serious injuries during this episode, and thankfully my parents no longer had me sleep in the top bunk! Later I did have a sleep-walking event that ended up in a trip to the Emergency Room. A fall down a flight of steps, broken nose, broken toe, stitches needed inside my mouth, and two really nice shiners were the result of that little stroll.

There were many other tales of my sleepwalking adventures. I never remembered any of the things I did while sleeping, which is very common with this condition. I feel kind of the same way now, when someone asks me what I did yesterday!

I may have digressed into the sleepwalking story, but in the dark and still of the night, I was letting the words flow to see where this would go. You, my dear reader, are experiencing the results.

An old legend from an unknown source says this: "Legend says, when you can't sleep at night, it's because you're awake in someone else's dream." Well, friends, I appreciate the thought, but please stop dreaming about me!!

May your brain and body get much needed rest every night. May you wake up refreshed, re-energized and renewed for the people who count on you. Sweet Dreams!! (Just leave me out of them!)

BLUE CHRISTMAS

STRANGE FEELINGS for me this year at holiday time. I am usually the person who starts the Christmas countdown in August...the one with the flashing lights necklace...the reindeer t-shirt...playing Christmas carols beginning in November...am all over the shopping and finding just the right thing for each person on my gift list. That's not me this year. I love the song "Blue Christmas" when Elvis sings it, but that is not normally my sentiment this time of year.

I don't have the same joy for Christmas music, events, decorations, shopping, baking and presents. Several times I have found myself thinking the words, "I don't care." It is all too much and not enough all at the same time. I am over it before it is over. I have never felt this way in my life.

Trying to analyze why I feel this way, I can come up with a number of reasons that might contribute to the blues. My dad died earlier this year and although we didn't have a huge celebration together, there is a puzzle piece missing where he fit in. It made me realize that for the most part, none of us know when we are having our last Christmas.

I had a rather large, milestone birthday this year. It was a number that reminded me there is less life in front of me than there is behind me. I have consciously acknowledged that I don't know how many sunrises I have left.

Christmas traditions have evolved and are vanishing as the dinosaurs did. My Christmas Eve traditions that have existed for my entire life are gone, completely gone. The people and places are gone, changed, absent.

It is a natural order of things, I understand that. A family moves away, marriages, births, deaths, the only constant in life is change. I guess it's been happening gradually, but this year seems to be the apex for me. I am looking over the mountain at the sunset side and nothing will ever be the same again. If you haven't stopped reading this tale of woe by now, you must be thinking what a cheery Christmas story this author tells!!

Let me reassure you, my light will continue to shine. I need to find new normals, new traditions and new reasons to embrace the season. Jesus is the reason for the season, and I am reminding myself of that daily. I am finding peace and calm playing familiar Christmas songs on my ukulele, a new skill I am learning. The unfamiliar coupled with the tried and true is working out pretty well.

So my promise to myself is to find new and joyful ways to embrace the Christmas season next year. I will find meaning in this spiritual season. I need to focus more on people I can help, and less on what I feel I have lost. Regardless of changes that are outside of my control, I have been blessed with so many wonderful family and friends in my life. Blessings that I take for granted are things other people are praying for.

> "There's a blessing behind every challenge, a door of opportunity for each window that closes, a rainbow after the rain. Weeping may last for the night, but His joy comes in the morning."
>
> — ADRIAN PANTONIAL, WRITER, EDITOR, LIFE COACH

May the grace and wisdom of God be with you during challenges and triumphs!

CHAPTER III
FAMILY AND FRIENDS

"Family is a life jacket in the stormy sea of life."

— J.K.ROWLING, AUTHOR

ORA'S ROLLING PIN

I HAVE WRITTEN ABOUT ORA, my great-grandma before. She was a great influence in my life even though I may not have realized it at the time. She was born in September, 1882. I don't know much about her life growing up, much to my dismay. I wasted so many opportunities to ask her questions and learn about her as a child, young girl, and then a bride.

I always enjoyed visiting her and watching her in the garden, the kitchen and at the sewing machine. She was frugal when times were tough, and could make much out of little. She did a lot of canning, baking, growing her own produce and sewing clothes for herself, and for me as her first great-grandchild. I like to think I was her favorite.

She made miracles in the kitchen. She had a wood cook-stove for most of her life, and most of the time I was growing up. She was an amazing cook, and made the best cookies you would ever want to eat.

One of the physical legacies I have is the rolling pin she used for many years. It is wooden, beautiful to look at, and quite hefty. Let's just say, I could be considered armed and dangerous with that beauty.

Whenever I take it out to use it, I think of her and feel connected to her and the things I learned from her. It is one of my most prized possessions.

My great-grandma Ora, lived to be 93. She was able to remain in her own home almost until the end of her life. I feel lucky that I got to have her in my life until my early twenties. Not many people get that much time to spend with a great-grandparent. I wish that I had a four generation picture of me, my mom, my grandma, and great-grandma. Maybe there was one taken, I just don't know about it or haven't come across it. Opportunities missed, but I have my memories.

ROMEO AND JULIET

WHO ISN'T familiar with the iconic story of the two star-crossed lovers? The tragedy, written by William Shakespeare in 1595, transcends time with its story of love, loss, and death. Most of us probably had to read the play at some point in our educational journey, maybe in a high school literature class. Review your iambic pentameter and give it another read!!

I often stayed with my cousin, Sandy, when I was growing up. She and her family lived on a farm near Cedar Rapids, Iowa. I didn't have any sisters, and she was an only child for the first nine years of her life. We were about the same age and became like sisters. We spent vacations, weekends, and summers staying at each other's houses and having adventures.

One summer when I was staying on the farm, my Aunt Barb decided to take us to the new movie that had just come out, *Romeo and Juliet, circa 1968.* I believe it was the first movie version of many to come. It was considered a movie that we were barely old enough to understand, but Barb deemed it appropriate for us to see.

It was a big day. We drove to downtown Cedar Rapids to the now iconic Paramount Theatre. It was the fanciest place I had ever visited. It was an enormous venue, multiple balconies, opulent decor, lots of red velvet, fancy seats, sconce lights, and more. Just viewing the inside of this place was a treat. The lights went down, and the movie began. Sandy and I were entranced by the love story playing out on the big screen. This movie became very popular with teens as the love story involved people close to our own age. There were tears, of course as the plot evolved and the story concluded. I have never forgotten this long ago day for a number of reasons. It was my first "grown-up" movie. My beloved Aunt Barb took me to see it along with my favorite cousin Sandy.

It was one of those experiences that made a deep impression on a young girl. Unfortunately, my Aunt Barb died at a very young age due to brain cancer of some sort. I have lots of memories of her, including the weeks she stayed with us as she underwent treatment at the University of Iowa

Hospital. She was a beautiful soul, that left a trail of light that will last forever. Her death changed the course of life for my cousin Sandy, her four-year-old brother, me and all those whose lives she had touched. Her earthly time was short, but her legacy is immense and continues today, many, many years later.

CHRISTMAS PAST

AHHH...THE years go by so swiftly. My great-grandmother used to say to me, "The days are long, but the years are fast." How true that has turned out to be, as I am older, hopefully, wiser and am looking back on my past. I prefer not to think of myself as old, I think of myself as chronologically gifted. (Not to mention gravitationally challenged, but that's another story...) I probably wouldn't notice my age, except my grandkids keep getting older, which is somewhat annoying. They are all in college or have graduated and are adulting and doing amazing things.

So my mind hearkens back to some of the Christmas traditions and fun when they were wee, small children. One of the traditions I started was how I wrapped their gifts. My oldest grandson, Tyler, is a person with Downs Syndrome. He wasn't reading yet but wanted to help pass out the presents with the other children. I decided to wrap each grandchild's present in a different wrapping, with no gift tags to read.

As they visited my house during the Christmas season, all the wonderful gifts under the tree, but nobody knew who they were for. At Christmas, when it was time to open gifts, I had a matching piece of gift wrap for each child, with their name and a Christmas greeting for them. That made it easy for everyone to deliver gifts to the appropriate recipient. I still do that today, I can't stop myself!!

A gift idea for the younger set; have a photograph of them made into a puzzle for them to put together. I ordered my puzzles online many years ago. I am sure you can find a producer of this personalized gift with a little research.

One last tradition, that I share with sadness in my heart. We had our Christmas tree in our living room. Our family Christmas festivities

took place in our downstairs family room that had a fireplace and was ginormous. So a second tree was a necessity. The downstairs tree was decorated entirely with candy. Candy canes, small chocolates that I could tape a ribbon on and hang on the tree. Bags of chocolate gold "coins" were nestled in the branches. It was topped with a Santa hat and a sign that proclaimed it the Grandpa Tree. Grandpa loved helping the children "undecorate" the tree and divide up the candy.

My husband, "Grandpa," died twelve years ago. I continued the Grandpa Tree tradition in his memory for all these years. The tree brought joy and sadness that this beloved Grandpa wasn't there to share in this tradition. This year will be the first year that there will be no Grandpa Tree. It is a hard decision, but it is time to file that memory in our hearts. I will always remember his delight in the Grandpa tree and his endless love for our delightful grandchildren.

Memories sustain us after the loss of a loved one. As long as we remember them, tell their story and keep them in our hearts, they still live. They are always with us and having them walk with us for part of our life's journey is a gift that no amount of money can purchase. To my husband: I have not heard your voice in years, but my heart has conversations with you often.

Make some memories with friends and family throughout the year. Celebrate each day and cherish those you love. John Greenleaf Whittier, an American Quaker Poet, wrote this "Of all sad words of tongue or pen, the saddest are these, 'It might have been." Let there be no "might have beens" in your life, make those memories, enrich your lives.

BICYCLES BUILT FOR THREE

THE SUMMER BEFORE SIXTH GRADE, my family was moving to a larger house, fortunately in the same school district. In fact, we moved right next door to Longfellow School, which we thought was pretty cool. One of the advantages was an entire playground full of slides, swings, jungle gyms, basketball hoops, monkey bars and the like.

My parents sold the swing set we had at our old house, and much to our surprise bought me and my brothers brand new bicycles. I hadn't had a new bike up to this point, learned and rode on hand-me-downs. My new bicycle was a sky blue Schwinn bike, with a white seat, streamers and a bell. It was the most beautiful thing I had ever seen. I don't really remember what my brother's bikes looked like, but I am sure they do.

We spent much time outside. If the day was nice, my mom would shoo us out the door, telling us "You are not houseplants." Bicycling was a huge part of our lives in those days. Our bicycles gave us freedom. We would jump on, take off, and the adventures would begin. If we were really on fire, we would attach playing cards to our spokes with clothespins. The noise they would make when we rode was very exciting, we pretended we were riding motorcycles. We could do a great deal with everyday objects and our imaginations. There were no limits to the dreams we dreamed, the lives we planned, and the friendships we formed. Life was ours, to invent, to dream, to play and to be kids. Sometimes...I wish I could rewind time, and go back to those days, to once more experience the play, the laughter, the exuberance and the joy of childhood.

I hope my parents knew how much joy they gave us with that unexpected gift of three bicycles...it was the ride of our lives!

GRAND OLD GAL

THERE ARE people in our lives, sometimes family, sometimes friends that change your life in small everyday moments, that last a lifetime. My Aunt Gladys was one of those people. She was my dad's aunt, sister to my grandmother, which made her my Grand (or Great) Aunt. Doesn't matter which title you prefer, she was both grand and great!!

We only lived about a dozen or so blocks from her and Uncle Jim in the first home my parents purchased. One of my strongest memories is riding my sky blue Schwinn bicycle over there on Saturdays to spend time with her. During those casual weekend hours, she taught me how to knit at the tender age of 9. She spent many hours guiding my young and clumsy hands until I could do a pretty consistent knit stitch and a purl stitch. Those two stitches are all you need to know to knit any pattern using different combinations. Those hours of learning gave me a skill that I remember and have used all of my life. I still knit today, and I think of Aunt Gladys every time!

She was also a wonderful cook and baker, and many treats were to be had at their house. I still use her pumpkin bread recipe today and it is a family favorite. Our family enjoyed many dinners at their home, simple times, having dinner, playing cards and "visiting."

She and Uncle Jim sometimes served as our babysitters when needed. I remember one night being taken to their house with my brother Randy, to spend the night as Mom and Dad headed to the hospital to bring our youngest brother, Bill into the world.

Another strong memory I have, was when she rescued my home economics project. She was a good seamstress. My first sewing project in junior high was to make an A-line skirt. Some of the work was done in class, but if not finished there, we had to do it at home.

My mom was not a seamstress, nor did we own a sewing machine. My finished skirt was due the next day. By due, I mean we had to wear our creations to school. It took us till late in the evening to fix and finish my skirt. She would be proud of me that I took up sewing at an older age, and am now an avid quiltmaker.

Aunt Gladys was a gentle, easygoing, sweet woman. She was the typical woman, wife, and mother of her era. She was the definition of a house-wife, in the 1950s and 60s. She always had a house dress on, complete with hose and wedge sandals. I never saw her wear pants until much later in her life.

She never learned to drive, which did make her dependent on her husband, my mom and others who would take her places. She was content to raise her son, mind the house, tend the garden and be a mentor and teacher to her nieces and nephews.

I have passed on what I learned from her. I have taught my nieces, grand-daughters and a number of young people how to knit. I bake her pumpkin bread in the autumn when pumpkin flavors dominate every kind of food. I have shared her recipe whenever possible, so many of my friends and family are out there making Aunt Gladys's pumpkin bread. (The recipe is in my first book, look for it there!!)

I was blessed in my life to have many aunts who cared for me, mentored me and were important parts of my life. An aunt makes life a little sweeter. They are teachers, mentors, mothers, friends, confidantes, cheerleaders and more. Recognize the aunts in your life and be grateful for the special gifts they have to share.

Definition of an aunt:

> "A cherished friend and personal cheerleader who will always see you through rose-colored glasses."
>
> — UNKNOWN

MOM ON THE RED CARPET

MY MOM and I were alike in some ways, our love of reading and books, shopping, going out for coffee, and our misadventures. My mom has been gone for eleven years, and unfortunately has missed out on some of my best stories.

Some many years ago, Julie Nixon Eisenhower, daughter of former President Nixon and granddaughter-in-law of former President Eisenhower was going to visit the Hoover Presidential Library and Museum to speak at the Hoover gravesite on the anniversary of President Hoover's birthday. My mom was very excited to go see Julie Eisenhower but wanted someone to go with her. My friend Deb's mother also wanted to go, so we connected them and plans were made to attend together.

Gelaine and Dot drove to West Branch without incident, (that we know of) parked and made their way to the gravesite area for the ceremony. The large grassy area was wet with morning dew. Why would you walk through that when there was this nice red carpet available to walk upon? Which they did, until such time as the Secret Service descended upon them and "helped" them off of the red carpet and into the crowd. Thus, paving the way for the guest of honor who was about to make her way down the red carpet. I can picture these two moms, their excitement, and then maybe a little chagrin as the scene unfolded.

This provided us with much laughter every time the subject came up. I joined in the laughter with mixed emotions, as this is sooooo something I could and would do. Since that time, I have had three interactions with the Secret Service, all delightful but those adventures are another story. My mother has one-upped me on this, however, as they never had to "remove" me from anywhere...yet.

TOOTH FAIRY — FACT OR FICTION?

ONCE UPON A TIME, many years ago, my granddaughter, Micaila had a close encounter concerning the Tooth Fairy. As is customary for many families, Micaila had been receiving money under her pillow when she lost a tooth. Nothing unusual about this, put the tooth under the pillow and wake up to find money in place of the tooth. Pretty slick, or so her mother thought.

Evidently, a tooth fairy discussion came up one day at school. A not so nice and somewhat worldly classmate informed Micaila that there was no such thing as a Tooth Fairy. In fact, to add insult to injury, she was informed that her mother was the Tooth Fairy. Micaila processed this information. She was a very bright girl, very logical and very literal.

Upon arriving home after school, she confronted her mother armed with new facts. She was going to get to the bottom of this. So she told her mother the things she had learned at school that day and sought confirmation. She bluntly said, "Mom, are you the Tooth Fairy?" Her mom processed this information, thinking, I am sure, that the innocence and magic of childhood can be so quickly destroyed, but she must be truthful. The time had come. So, she responded, "Yes, Micaila, I am the Tooth Fairy." Micaila was blown away by this new truth. She said, "You are the Tooth Fairy? For everybody?" I think she was awed and surprised by this enormous and heretofore unknown title that belonged to her mom. Well, unfortunately, her mom was not as cool as Micaila thought for that one brief glorious moment.

Our family was very amused by this turn of events, and this marvelous Micaila growing up story. Micaila believed.

❝ "Those who don't believe in magic will never find it."

— ROALD DAHL

MENDING A BROKEN HEART

SITTING HERE WRITING TODAY, waiting for periodic updates as my brother, Randy, has heart surgery. Not an emergency procedure, scheduled, but worrisome nonetheless. The irony of him needing a heart by-pass and a valve repaired overwhelms me. He is trim and fit, works out, a 50-mile bicycle ride is nothing for him, and he climbs 11 flights of steps to his office regularly.

He has been somewhat angry about this, and I don't blame him. He has done everything right, yet here he is, about ready to have his chest opened up and his heart in the hands (literally) of surgeons and other medical staff. Here I sit, three years older, twenty pounds overweight, not a fan of working out, ride my bicycle for twirls around the neighborhood, and you would have to drag me to get me up eleven flights of steps. Who knows...I too may need this done as we have a history of family heart disease.

Heredity is a strong factor in many aspects of our lives and our health.

As a former chairperson of the American Heart Association, Go Red for Women in our area, I am well informed about heart disease. Excuse this small infomercial, but it may help you or someone you know.

Heart disease is the number one killer of Americans period. All types of cancer added together still don't beat the number of deaths from heart disease. Be aware, particularly if you are female. Heart disease can present different symptoms in women than in men. If something doesn't seem right, go to the doctor, keep going, advocate for yourself.

Don't take no for an answer, until you get something definitive from your medical personnel. Make sure your doctor is someone who listens to you and your concerns. Don't take part in an assembly line medical appointment.

My brother had no symptoms, so he is lucky to have this discovered before a cardiac event occurred. He has been told repeatedly by medical personnel that his fitness and good health will help him on the other side of surgery for a quicker recovery. He is tired of hearing that!!

So, we wait for updates, praying that all is going well. May God guide the hands of the surgeon, watch over my brother during surgery and after, and lead him to a good outcome and speedy recovery.

> "Open heart surgery is now part of a typical life experience for many people. Folks talk casually about "having a stent put in," as if they had their tires rotated."
>
> — ROGER EBERT, AMERICAN FILM CRITIC

Well, Mr. Ebert, I have had my tires rotated, (more than once!) and it didn't change my life. It is not casual if it is you or a loved one having the surgery, funny as your remark might seem!

And we wait…

(Update: Randy came through the surgery beautifully and is back to all of his activities.)

CHIMING IN

THINKING ABOUT MY MOM TODAY, who has been gone for eleven years now.

The quality of her health and therefore life had deteriorated the last four years of her life. She had been battling diabetes and heart disease for a number of years, and it had been taking its toll on her body. There were numerous trips to the emergency room, followed by hospital stays of various lengths of time. She was a trooper and did her best not to let it affect her spirit and her enjoyment of her life. She always befriended her nurses, sometimes playing pranks on them.

Then there came yet another emergency room visit, and as my mind contemplated her condition and the words of the doctors, I came to a realization. I went to the doctor who was entering information on his computer, and asked him this simple question: "Is my mom here this time to die?" He didn't answer yes or no, how could he? Only God knows the time and place that our earthly journey will end. My mom was a fighter and had surprised the doctors on more than one occasion. He only said quietly, "She is a very sick woman."

It was a long five weeks. I am so glad I was able to be with her almost every day, and be an advocate for her care as she was no longer able to do that for herself. There was some unpleasantness in taking on this role of advocate, which included me educating a thoughtless, arrogant nurse who spoke sharply to my mom. I followed her out of the room and asked her if she had actually looked at my mom's file. At that time, a patient's medical records were in paper form, in a binder that went with them everywhere in the hospital. Her binder was thicker than a New York City phone book back in the day of landlines. As I dressed down the nurse, her response to me was: "Well, I didn't know how sick she was, some people like to come here for a little vacation." That remark did not shorten my attempt to educate her!! There may have been smoke coming out of my head!

I also wrote a letter that I left with my mom, to give any doctor since I had yet to speak to anyone. The "hospitalist," (a new and very unsatisfying way of caring for hospitalized patients less expensively while cutting their personal physicians out of the picture) never came when I was there. In the letter, among other things, I asked who, if anybody, was in charge of her care. I was steamed and it was a long letter. Evidently, it got someone's attention, and they moved her from a generalist floor to the cardiac floor to a private room. The nurses and doctors on that floor were amazing, knew her from her many visits, and cared for her in a compassionate way.

I brought her little surprises frequently, which wasn't easy. She could no longer enjoy much of anything. The best gift I brought her was a wind chime. We hung it from the ceiling where she could see it. The nurses and visitors got in the habit of giving it a gentle push when they went in and out of the room. Mom had a number of wind chimes at home and enjoyed this gift very much. I highly recommend this as a gift to someone who is hospitalized. It is longer lasting than flowers, and the joyful sound of the chimes is a welcome melody to all.

So it came to pass, this was her final hospital stay. Her life had shrunk to this hospital room, with no hope for more. She expressed that she wanted to die and was ready. She passed away in the hospital and was finally at peace. The nurses knew the signs when it was her time. They had gentle music playing and lit a candle. My dad and I were there to say our last good-bye.

I also have a love of windchimes and have several at my home. I often think of my mom when the wind blows and I hear the chimes, speaking to me. My mom and I didn't always agree about things, but as I near the age when she died, I understand that no matter their age, you worry about your children and want the best for them.

My mom was a spirited woman who loved to read, ride her moped (which was large enough you had to have a motorcycle license to ride it!) shop, and enjoyed winters in Florida and Arizona. She was an Avon lady for many years and often delivered orders to her customers on the aforementioned moped. Many people around Iowa City knew her or of her because of this!!

Author Susie Clevenger said this, "A breeze twists the wind chimes into a song breaking my heart with the melody of your absence." It does do that at times, but also brings me joy and memories of my mom.

One of my greatest disappointments is that she did not live to see me write and publish my books. She would have loved that, and been very proud of me. If there is a bookstore in heaven, (and how could there not be, if it's heaven??) I am sure she has acquired copies of both of my books, and would certainly have some editorial remarks for me!!

If my wind chimes are creating a riotous noise outside as I write this, I am guessing it's her!! Thinking of you, Mom and wishing you were here.

> "If I had a flower for every time I thought of you, I could walk in my garden forever."
>
> — ALFRED TENNYSON, POET LAUREATE OF GREAT BRITAIN

Take a walk in that garden, listen for the wind chimes, and breathe in the sweet scent of the flowers planted there and give thanks for the loved ones who shared part of the journey of your life.

PINK STATION WAGON

AS A SOCIALLY ACTIVE, energetic and flourishing high schooler, I was always on the go. School, a job at Hy-Vee, extracurricular activities, social events, and a boyfriend or two found me busily buzzing around town. My parents had to bear the burden of most of the transportation initially. So my hardworking dad decided I needed my own car to transport myself, and also my younger brothers. The latter part did not thrill me, but what's a girl gonna do?

Dad began the car search by having his friend Carl, in Wellman, Iowa keep his eye out for something dependable at a reasonable cost. Carl owned an auto repair garage and often heard about cars that might be for sale. One day, Dad shows up driving my "new" car. It was a 1962 pink Plymouth station wagon. My dad thought he was pretty funny with his choice of car for me. My initial reaction was lukewarm, but hey, I had a car now.

Here is where the fun begins...first of all, the car had a push-button transmission. On the left side of the steering wheel, there was a vertical row of buttons labeled: Reverse, Neutral, Drive, First, Second. To engage the transmission there was a lever to pull up (taking the car out of park), and then pushed the appropriate button to put it in gear. Very cool.

There was one consideration in purchasing this car that may have escaped my dad's attention, as he was too busy laughing about me driving a pink station wagon. Do you have any idea how many teenagers you can pile into a station wagon pre-seatbelt law days? Allegedly, I may have transported 12-14 friends on several occasions. Oh, the stories that car could tell.

One day, my dad's truck was in the shop. He needed to borrow mine to go to work. That night at dinner, he commented that while driving the car around town, all kinds of people were honking at him. He was perplexed and I didn't say a word. Sometimes, you just need to smile, nod, and keep quiet! My car was very well known around the metroplex of Iowa City and Coralville. It is not every day you see a nine or ten-year-old pink station wagon on the loose.

I put a lot of miles on that car, gas was 36 cents a gallon. If I had a dollar in my pocket, I was on the road! I have such good memories of that car. I am smiling as I write this, thinking of the days of my youth and the adventures with the Pink Plymouth. If I could buy a restored version of this car, I would buy it in a New York minute.

Lyrics by Mary Hopkins from a well-known song come to mind:

"Those were the days my friend. We thought they'd never end. We'd sing and dance forever and a day. We'd live the life we'd choose, we'd fight and never lose for we were young and sure to have our way."

I will never forget those days, those friends, those adventures and my special pink car. Millions of memories, thousands of jokes, hundreds of secrets...those WERE the days my friends.

Round up some special memories, share them with friends and family. The past adventures of our life helped shape the person we are today. Pay the proper respect to your memories, dust them off and share them with the world every now and then.

TEA WITH ALLISON

WHEN MY GRANDDAUGHTER Allison was somewhere in the age range of three to five years old, she loved her tea parties. I had purchased a china tea set in a wicker basket that also had a soft doll in it to have tea with. I kept this at my house for something special to do when she stayed with us.

Allison loved to have tea parties with me and her grandpa. Well, she called them tea parties, but she ran them more like she was the CEO of Amazon. There were rules and certain behavior was not only expected but required. She would serve apple juice or water from her teapots and fill our china cups. "Crumpets" were served on the tiny plates. I taught her that word, and it encompassed anything I had available to give her to use: goldfish crackers, M & M's, jelly beans, etc. They all became crumpets when they were placed on the tea plates!

Grandpa liked to do silly things, like wear his napkin on his head, or slurp rudely and loudly out of his teacup. Allison would put her hand on her hip, give him her most indignant look and say, "Grandpa, take that off your head, or you can't have any more tea." But she would follow that up with, "You only get five more chances!" Her love for Grandpa and her soft side overruled the occasional lapses and tricks he would play.

Allison has grown into a lovely young woman, attending college and working toward her goals. I still have the tea party set and doll, which will be hers whenever she wants it. God willing, maybe I will get to have tea parties with her daughter someday

I hope you have a chance to attend a tea party. I hope someone loves you enough to give you only "five more chances," and I hope you take the time today to make some memories with someone you love.

RECONNECTIONS

I HAVE RECENTLY RECONNECTED with a long-time friend, Deb. I would say an old friend, but she will read this and I would pay! Let's just say we are chronologically gifted. We have known each other since junior high but became best friends in high school. By best friends, I really mean there was a small group of us that were inseparable. We have lots of stories, adventures, antics, and events that are legendary but known only to us. Some of those things could have ended up badly, but we were lucky. We were young, full of oats that needed to be sowed. It was a simpler, safer time to come of age than it is now. If we weren't together, we were on the phone planning the next slumber party. We wore each other's clothes without a thought. Deb actually ran away from home in high school after an argument with her dad and lived with my family for a couple of weeks. I was the maid of honor in her wedding, and am godmother to one of her children. How do friends that are so connected become out of touch?

The answer is simple, I don't know how that happens. There wasn't a single event, it was a slow withdrawal from each other. We were separated due to life's complexities, circumstances and poor communication. We were at different places in our marriages, and in our lives. There was no break-up, no giving back of the virtual friendship bracelets, and no custody battle over mutual friends.

We have recognized our divide, and are recovering, rebuilding and renewing the bonds that joined us in the first place. It is a slow process. It is joyful to laugh about the shared memories that only we have. It is hysterical to laugh about the aging process that has and is happening to us. It is tearful to talk about friends and family who have left us to go to their eternal home.

The distance must be overcome to complete this process of restoring friendship. In some cases, it may be geographical distance, or it may be an emotional distance. Distance is distance and steps must be taken to close that space between you until it is no longer.

The friendship is still there, always has been. It has been dormant like a hibernating bear. Spring has arrived and the bear is awakening...so watch out!! There may be some more adventures to have and memories to make. Our lunch dates last over two hours and most of it is spent laughing and sharing.

Eleanor Roosevelt, former First Lady had this to say, "Many people will walk in and out of your life, but only true friends leave footprints in your heart."

On your journey today, take attendance. Who is not showing up in your life that should be? Who is just taking up space and is not really a true friend? Recognize, reach out, rebuild, recover, renew and restore the relationships that make your life special. It will be a gift you give yourself to treasure for all time.

MY MOTHER'S RING

As I write this, today would have been my mom's 85th birthday, but she is celebrating in heaven and has been for eleven years. This year my dad has joined her, so I hope she had a wonderful day. In honor of her birthday, I wore her ring, which is a gold band with five diamonds. I am wearing a couple of generations of history, and an interesting tale.

My mother's first marriage was at a young age, and short-lived, and I was a product of that marriage. She later married the man that I called Dad. He adopted me when I was four and was the only dad I ever knew growing up. I knew at the age of four I was adopted. I didn't really understand what it meant, but to me, it meant I was special...I know, big surprise. My delusions of grandeur raising its' ugly head at a tender age.

So my mom had two diamond rings from her marriages. When my maternal and paternal grandmothers passed away, she ended up with their diamond rings as well. What does one do with four diamond rings? It is rather difficult to wear them all at once. Do you put them on a rotation?? My mom had a different idea, she had all those diamonds, and a new one that she added made into a new ring, which is the one I inherited from her, and wear frequently.

When I wear the ring, it is hard not to think about the women that wore these rings, and the men who gave them. I treasure this ring, and all that it means to me, and what it meant to the women who went before me. The ring connects me to them.

> "I am bound to them even though I cannot look into their eyes or hear their voices. I honor their history. I cherish their lives. I will tell their story. I will remember them."

> — Author Unknown

REFLECTIONS

I HAVE BEEN SITTING beachside at the Gulf of Mexico for about two weeks. During one of these sand, sun, and sea sessions, I received a phone call that changed my life. It wasn't an unexpected phone call, it was from my brother, Bill, telling me that our father had passed away. Dad had been in Hospice Care at a wonderful place called The Bird House. He had been fairly stable and I thought he would still be there in his cozy nest when I returned from my trip. Not meant to be. He is at peace in his forever home and reunited with my mother at long last.

About a week before I left, he looked at me and said, "I miss your mother terribly." He was so quiet and sad as he said this, and tears came quickly to my eyes. He was not a man to show his feelings, and I had never heard him say anything like this during the eleven years since my mother died. I replied, "Dad, I think you will see her soon." His face lit up with a light I thought was long gone. He had the joy of a seven-year-old who has just been told, "You're going to Disney World!" He said, "Really? Is she coming here?" I said, "No, Dad, you are going to see her." He seemed very content and I hope he carried that conversation in his heart until he was called home on February 14th, Valentine's Day. I choose to believe he wanted to be with Mom on the day that celebrates love. They were married for fifty-one and a half years. I am sure it was a joyous reunion.

The ocean has given me peace these days while I am processing the death of my father. The rhythm and repetition of the waves are calming and mesmerizing. The last few days the waves have been extremely exuberant, leaving piles of seashells, the ocean's treasures. The seascape is so different from my home in the gently rolling hills of Iowa, but it is bringing me peace for the days and rest for the nights until I return home.

GENERATIONAL LOSS

FEELING ISOLATION, letdown, and loss. The final services for my dad were a few days ago. It was a nice tribute to his life and provided some closure for my brothers and me, as well as other family and friends. So, why don't I feel more at peace? The loss of a second parent closes the door on that generation of your family. My brothers and I are now either the glue that holds the family together, or we are the loose-leaf notebook that doesn't close properly and all the papers scatter in the wind. It's a scary responsibility.

As my brothers and I examined old pictures and the belongings of my dad, we had lots of questions. I have already had thoughts of regrets in the past, regarding questions I didn't ask my mom, grandparents, and great-grandparents. Now I can add my dad to the list. Even though Dad was having some memory issues during the last year, it was his short term memory that he struggled with. His memories of the past were as clear as a newly cleaned window. We witnessed some of that as he visited with his twin brother for the last time, and reminisced about their history growing up together.

One of the questions I have been pondering is my dad's military service. He was drafted at the tender age of eighteen. He was one of five brothers on the farm near a very small town in rural Iowa. Uncle Sam wanted four of the five. I wonder what emotions he must have felt. He was a farm boy, probably had never traveled more than fifty miles from his farm, when he found himself in the middle of the Pacific Ocean on his way to a foreign land. Destination: Japan, a country that less than ten years earlier had had bombed Pearl Harbor. Unlike today, he did not have the internet or television to provide information about the world. I can't even begin to process what he must have been feeling. Homesickness, fear, loneliness, and isolation to name a few.

It is a mystery to me why I didn't think about these questions when he could have answered them. Is it because we cease to recognize our parents as people who had whole lives before we existed? Is it the closer examination of his life and possessions? I am sad for the apparent lack of curiosity

I exhibited before he passed away. We think we know our parents, after all, haven't we spent our whole lives interacting with them? The tricky part is that we only know them as parents, not as people who were once young with adventures, hopes, dreams, fears, doubts, love and heartbreak.

For my readers who still have parents and grandparents, ask the questions. Write down the answers to share with other family members. Ask about historical events that affected their lives. What was it like to grow up in that time and place? Take the opportunities that I neglected and explore the early lives of those generations before you. It will be a treasure beyond value.

SALES TAX ... WHAT??

SOME YEARS AGO, my grandson Josh was spending the day with me and as usual, we had big plans for big adventures. He and his sister Allison loved it when we wrote out an itinerary of what the day would entail. She particularly liked crossing things off after we accomplished them. As a senior in college, she is still a list maker like her grandmother.

On this particular occasion, Josh had saved some money and we were going to go shopping. Josh was always a careful shopper, he took his time when deciding what to buy, and was very aware of how much money he had and the cost of the items he was looking for. After much deliberation, he made his choice and we headed to the cashier to make his purchase. That is where the trouble began…

The cashier rang up his purchase and said, "That will be $10.40. The look of dismay on his face was painful. He looked at me for validation as he said, "That's not right the sign said it was $10.00." I then explained the concept of sales tax to a very unhappy eight-year-old. He listened but was not convinced. He said, "I don't want to pay that. I want to pay $10.00." I told him that none of us "want" to pay the sales tax, but we don't have a choice. He was very indignant and after a little more discussion about economics and the unfairness of life, I said I would pay the sales tax. (It's what grandmothers do!)

Always educational and thought-provoking to see the world through the eyes of a child of any age. Spending time with children is certainly more important than spending money on them, but once in a while, a little financial boost saves the day. Will Rogers, (American Humorist) once said, "The quickest way to double your money is to fold it over and put it back in your pocket." Especially if they ask you to pay sales tax...

A GAME WITH AUTHORS

Ahh...the games people play, or more importantly the games children play. Growing up, my family played a lot of cards and board games. My brothers and I often played games, particularly when we were in elementary school. One family tradition that encouraged this, happened at Christmas. Of course, we were beyond excited about the gifts under the tree, and often begged to open one early. My mom started the practice of letting us open one joint gift a day or two before the deal happened. It would be a new game for us to play to keep us busy (and out of her hair) in the days before Christmas.

One of those early Christmas gifts was a game that has stayed in my mind since those long-ago days, is the card game of Authors. This game was first published in 1897 by Parker Brothers, and still stands the test of time today. The cards in the deck consisted of famous authors in sets of four, with a different literary work by them on each card. The object was to collect sets of four, and the player with the most complete sets of authors won.

We had no idea at the time, the significance and weight of the authors whose names we tossed out casually as if we were playing Go Fish. Some of the authors in the game were Louisa May Alcott, Henry Wadsworth Longfellow, James Fenimore Cooper, Sir Walter Scott, Mark Twain, William Shakespeare, Charles Dickens, Washington Irving, Robert Louis Stevenson, and Nathaniel Hawthorne. When I hear those names today, I am taken back to that day and time and the names we knew by heart, though we knew not the importance of their writings.

We had a special affinity for Henry Longfellow, as we attended Longfellow elementary school. The poem by Longfellow, "The Song of Hiawatha," still resonates with me.

> "On the shores of Gitche Gumee,
> Of the shining Big- Sea -Water,
> Stood Nokomis, the old woman,
> Pointing with her finger westward,

O'er the water pointing westward,
To the purple clouds of sunset.."

An extremely lengthy poem, that is really a story, and what kid wouldn't want to recite the words: "Gitchee Gumee??"

Other card games we played are also still in use today. I speak of "Old Maid," and "War." The great thing about War was it didn't take any strategy or skill, other than knowing how to count, and which cards were a higher value. It really was luck of the draw, but fun nonetheless.

Board games included Candy Land, Chutes and Ladders, Clue and Monopoly. God bless the adults in our life who suffered through countless games of Candy Land with us!

A child's full-time occupation should be playing. They learn, they stretch their imagination, they socialize, they engage, they have fun.

Albert Einstein, theoretical physicist, who was also somewhat of a philosophist said, "Play is the highest form of research." I would say children and adults alike should engage in a little more research!

THE ELEPHANT IN THE ROOM

I JUST RETURNED from dinner with some very dear friends, who also happen to be work colleagues...or they were. Two of them are moving on to explore different job opportunities. One of them, Nancy, is moving several hours away for her new job.

Our dinners, road trips, and adventures are legendary. We laugh till we cry, and we cry until we can laugh again. Tonight's dinner was no different. There was hilarity, conversation, reminiscing and the solving of world and local problems. However, tonight's dinner was different. It was the last time we would all be together before the "move." None of us mentioned it, but it was definitely the elephant in the room.

Our friendship will endure the test of distance, but it will be different. The adventures or dinners out won't be spontaneous. It will take effort and planning to make it work. We not only have to deal with the busy calendars of everyone in the group but the miles which separate us. Every member of the group will have to be "all in" to keep the group together and viable.

Nancy is a special friend to me. She has been in the trenches with me when I couldn't see a way to climb out. She brought the ladder and a helping hand. She has encouraged and supported my endeavors. She appreciates my idiosyncrasies and embraces them. She particularly likes my ability to crack myself up. I must admit, I enjoy this ability myself.

When I left dinner, I had a funny feeling in the pit of my stomach. It wasn't good-bye, it was, see you later. But I knew at that moment a transition had started and things would never be quite the same again. Life is full of changes, and we are not always the captain of that boat, but we stay on board and enjoy the ride. The Friend*ship* doesn't always provide a turbulence-free cruise, but the rewards are worth the trip. I will always buy the ticket and take that ride.

William Shakespeare said, "Words are easy, like the wind. Faithful friends are hard to find." Take a look around your life today, appreciate the friends who add value to your life, laughter to your days and are always ready to join your next adventure.

LEMON MERINGUE PIE

It is delightful to be able to make desserts for your family and loved ones. Baking is an act of love for me. There is also something therapeutic about baking from scratch recipes, no boxes or quick fixes. (Don't get me wrong, I am all about those when needed!) So when my son-in-law Wes, asked me if I knew how to make a lemon meringue pie, I needed to learn how. I have never made one, but am always willing to try new recipes.

I am the youngest of five sisters-in-law in the family I married into. The other four are farm wives, great cooks and I like to turn to them for cooking tips among other things. So, with hope in my heart, I emailed my sister-in-law Julie (sorry Julie) and asked her if she had a good recipe for lemon meringue pie. She responded quickly in a return email. Here is her response:

"Yes, I do."

1. Get in your car.
2. Go to Village Inn.
3. Buy a lemon meringue pie.
4. Take it home and serve it.

This still makes me laugh, every time I read it. I printed it out, taped it to a recipe card and filed it in my recipe box under Pies. This is why I go to my sisters-in-law with questions and concerns. They are wise in the ways of the world and quick to help me. They share their family recipes without hesitation. On a serious note, these women have been a great support to me, welcomed me to the family with no reservations (they didn't know me that well then…) and have always been there for me. Color me blessed, and thanks to Julie, my lemon meringue pies are the best around…

PARTY IN A BOX

As a child, birthdays were a pretty big deal for me. Lots of attention, exclamations over my age, grandparents, taking birthday treats to school, presents, and parties. Birthdays are still a big deal to me, unfortunately, at my age, nobody else really cares!!

For a number of my birthdays, my mom ordered a special cake for me. It was a round layer cake or angel food cake. In the center of the cake, there would be a Barbie doll, and the cake was decorated to look like her dress. The dress, of course, was a flowing ball gown with swirls and flourishes. The dream cake for many little girls. I loved those cakes.

Reminiscing with friends about this cake, one of my good friends, Debby, confessed she had never had one of these cakes and always wanted one. Her birthday was approaching, so I filed that away in one of the dusty corners of my mind to see if I could find her a Barbie doll cake.

Plans were made for the gang to go to our favorite pizza place, Herb & Lou's. This restaurant/bar is in the city of West Branch, home of President Herbert Hoover. For those of you in the dark, his wife's name was Lou...Hence, the restaurant's name.

I was able to order a Barbie doll cake from our local grocery store, Hy-Vee. If memory serves me right, I had to provide the doll. When I went to pick up the cake on the night of the party, it was even better than I anticipated. Not only was the cake magnificent, the packaging was also amazing. The cake was in a beautiful box with handles. The printing on the outside proclaimed, "Party in a Box." Allegedly, I may

have said at some point in the past, "I bring the party." Well, hallelujah, now I have proof. I was beyond excited to meet up with my friends, carrying a party in a box!!

The presentation of the cake was at the end of the evening that was filled with pizza, beer, laughter, friendship, and silliness. Debby was excited about her cake and many photos were taken!! There was a lot of cake so we shared it with the cooks and servers at the restaurant and that made the celebration even better. I have to confess, I really wanted to keep that box and carry it around like a purse, but once in a while, my common sense and good judgment do kick in! As my granddaughter, Allison said to me when she was about 10, "Grandma, just because you can, doesn't mean you should." I remind myself of that advice...maybe not often enough!

Henry Wadsworth Longfellow, American poet and educator said, "And the song, from beginning to end, I found again in the heart of a friend."

May your friends stand by your side, in good times and bad. May they help you sing that song in your heart when you've forgotten the tune.

CHAPTER IV

PLACES AND FACES

"Favorite people, favorite places, favorite memories of the past. These are the joys of a lifetime, these are the things that last."

— Henry van Dyke, Dutch American author, poet and educator

COMMAND CENTRAL

MY COFFEE TABLE is where it all happens. At any moment, it may be covered with papers, knitting, books. checkbook, ukulele, journal, book pages, notecards, pens, remotes, phone, laptop, and iPad. I could run the country from here. Based on the national news some days, I should be running the country. Admittedly, I am the sole cause and creator of this hot mess, and it does not make me happy, nor am I running the country. Two strikes.

It is handy while watching television as a prop for putting my legs up, holding a cold beverage and the remote control. On the other hand, it becomes a catch-all for whatever I am working on, reading, and a plethora of other objects. It is painful to look at, and completely my fault.

For family Christmas, it gets moved out of the way to make more floor space for people and presents. I love how open and clean my living room looks when it is gone. Do I really need to put my feet up while watching TV? However, where would all the very important, critical to life as I know it, "stuff" go? Let's be honest, we all know it is going to end up somewhere! If I let my very significant gentleman friend have a vote, it is staying. He is very fond of the "serves as a leg-rest" feature of the coffee table. I guess it has to stay, but my love-hate relationship with it will continue.

If your coffee table is not as well equipped as mine, you can always purchase a dust collector, oops, I mean coffee table book. Books made for the purpose of having them lie on a table that purports to be for the purpose of drinking coffee. These are the kinds of topics that tickle my fancy. It reminds me of another favorite; reading a book about how to write a book. These are certainly not the thoughts that stir men's souls, but they do stir my imagination and sense of humor.

LOW TIDE ADVENTURES

I AM WELL aware that some of my stories run amok and seem to have a life of their own. In case you are wondering about the title, no, I am not running low on laundry detergent! This is a low tide adventure on the beach this morning. We decided to get up at a serious O:Dark-Thirty time, low tide, to see what treasures the ocean had left us during the night. We did have to wait a bit after low tide because it was too dark to even see!!

We scurried down to the beach in the quiet, semi-darkness, excited to examine the bounty that the ocean had surely left us. It didn't take too long on our walk down the beach for disappointment to set in. The leavings from the ocean this early morning were small. We could see the line all the way down the beach, a small curvy line of shells that were left. There is one way I can describe the detritus. It looked as if God had swept his kitchen of the crumbs and dust into a tidy pile, and still needed to get his dustpan out for the final step. The shells or parts of shells were very tiny, and sparse.

Surprised and a little disappointed after our very eager, early morning awakening that we would reap nothing for our efforts. But the beach was very peaceful, the ocean sounds, quiet and melodic, provided the background music for our walk. It was nice when the adventure became about the walk, the sights, sounds, and smell of the ocean. The soft sand underfoot, sandpipers scurrying around at water's edge, the mesmerizing sound of the waves bouncing gently against the shore, and the gentle breeze cooling my face bring me peace. In all honesty, it wasn't about finding new shells for me, it was about the adventure of being up and about before the day began and seeing what it was all about. I have been coming to this beach area for more than two decades, I DO NOT need to bring home shells!!!

I have always been fascinated by the ocean tides and the magnetic pull of the moon that controls them. It is one of those facts that makes me stop and ponder the magnificence of this world and the One who created it. The unceasing, never-ending, eternal ebb and flow of the ocean is melodic, comforting and yet somewhat incomprehensible to a mere mortal like me.

The earth's rotation and the relationship with the moon, sun and other stars is a pleasant mystery to me. I know just a little, and that is enough. I don't have to understand it to appreciate it and be pleased and mystified by it!

There are so many metaphors about tides/water and life. Of course, water is life for us in so many ways. The human body is made up of about 60% water. We need to drink water to survive, literally. We need to bathe in water to not offend those who must live in close proximity to us. We are drawn to water. If there is a body of water, no matter how small, there will be people around it. It fascinates us, it calls to us.

> "The ocean stirs the heart, inspires the imagination, and brings eternal joy to the soul."
>
> — ROBERT WYLAND, AMERICAN ARTIST.

Such true words, I feel once you see the majesty of an ocean, you are forever changed.

On your journey, have a low tide adventure, look at an ocean, ponder your connection to it, drink it in and let it fill your heart, mind, and soul.

HIGH ANXIETY

PLANNING a get-away is usually a medley of high energy, gleeful anticipation, research, and itineraries. This particular planning event wasn't quite what we expected. We had been discussing a fall trip, but we had not even penciled anything in. Over coffee, that suddenly changed. We made a rather impromptu and rapid decision to travel to Boston, in two weeks.

In a couple of hours, we had plane tickets booked, and were gleefully gloating. The gloating quickly changed to glumness, and then for me, high anxiety struck. In attempting to book a hotel room, starting with the hotel we had previously occupied in Boston, we were confronted with a rude awakening. Hotels were very full or sold out. To add insult to injury, the nightly rates were being quoted as $1,000 and up. When informed of this turn of events, I replied to Verne with the comment, "Did you tell them we just want to sleep there, not purchase the room?" After several hours of searching, he indicated he was done for the day. I picked up the torch and ran.

Evidently, it was the high season in Boston. Hayden Fry, legendary Iowa football coach would have wondered if they were having a "high porch picnic." Peak leaf season, the Red Sox were back for a homestand, and goodness knows what else was going on. So, high season, high prices, high porch picnic, and for me high anxiety.

After much more stress and research, I did find a hotel in Back Bay.

The prices were better, and still only a mile from the Boston Commons and the hub of activity in Boston. An easy walk or ride on the "T" would get us there. Bonus fact: we are closer to Fenway, so if we score baseball tickets that will be an easy walk.

We do not belong, nor do we aspire to join the $1000+++ a night hotel club. Our needs are simple. A clean room, comfortable bed and the normal amenities hotels provide are all we ask for. We don't spend that much time in our room, as we want to experience all that our travel destination has to offer. We may leave the room for breakfast and not return until late evening.

For the prices they were asking in Boston proper I would expect breakfast in bed, a personal hairstylist, wine, snacks, new magazines, cookies and milk, and a signed deed showing we now owned the room in said hotel. It seems like a fair trade to me.

Travel can be costly, so planning and research certainly help keep the costs down. Choosing to travel, rather than to purchase "things," no matter the cost, is owning an experience. It is yours for the rest of your life. Looking at it that way, the value is incalculable.

J.R. R. Tolkien, English author, and poet said this: "Still around the corner, there may wait, a new road or a secret gate." Travel, exploration, new places, new faces, the possibility of finding that new road or a secret gate will propel us to the next adventure, over and over again.

One doesn't have to travel far, there are many hidden treasures and wonderful places nearby, we just have to look for them.

SIXTH-GRADE GLIMPSES FROM AN OCCASIONAL TEACHER

IN MY YEARS of impromptu performances as a guest teacher, I must confess that secretly (well, not anymore) sixth grade has been my favorite grade level. This is a sweet, funny, ridiculous, ornery, lovable and curious age. They are on the cusp of changing into teenagers and young adults. They are pretty transparent and will rat each other out at the drop of a hat, and yet will still be best friends ten minutes later. Here are some glimpses from my perspective.

The girl who wanted a hug every morning from the teacher.

The boy who pulled me aside to tell me he had a very bad cold, and he thought I would like to know that.

The boys that gathered at my desk to talk about the Hawkeye game last Saturday, and to tell me jokes.

The girls that lingered at my desk to admire my jewelry, show me their dress, barrettes, haircut, or to give me a flower.

The girl that came in sobbing from recess because another student told her she was the reason her parents were getting a divorce.

The boys who plaster their faces and arms with scotch tape when I am not looking are the same boys who put paper bags over their heads when I pass out bags for a charitable drive.

The boy who wondered out loud if my husband and I were going to the Penn State game in Happy Valley that we might take him. Followed by, "Well, maybe that would be weird cuz we're not related or anything."

The boy who asked me in the hallway if I would be his Grandma.

The students who ask me to spell words for them as they are typing an essay...and are amazed that I know how to spell lots of words. One young gentleman asked me if I could spell all the words in the dictionary. I replied, "Yes." I mean, it's not like he is going to give me a test!

I enjoy them all, and I must admit I do get a kick out of the ornery students, as long as it's funny and not mean or disrespectful. Some days it is very difficult to keep a straight face, as the classroom seems like a comedy hour...all day long!

Adam Sandler, actor/comedian said, "Sixth grade was a big time, in my childhood, of hoops and friendship, and coming up with funny things." I too remember my sixth-grade year with fond memories of Mrs. Griffith reading aloud "The Trumpeter of Krakow," to us, Mrs. George letting me help in the library, recess, books, and many friends, some of whom are still in my life today. Those were the days...

CHARACTERS IN OUR LIVES

Aннн...тне people that populate our lives. I like to think of them as characters in a novel getting to know them, being surprised and enjoying the "read." One of my favorite things is meeting new people. I am not talking about cocktail parties, mix and mingles, or planned social events. I am very fond of the serendipitous meetings. Characters that come into my life in unplanned ways: travel, coffee shops, diners, the post office. Today, I had one of those meetings.

I was writing at my normal coffee shop, my first outing after being very under the weather for the last week. I finally have energy, I need to get out amongst the hoi polloi and see my peeps!! My favorite barista Sarah welcomes me and gets me my first of any number of drinks I may imbibe here, depending on how the writing goes which determines how long I stay. Today, it is also dependent on my energy level, which I am testing after having been under house arrest so to speak!!

Sarah is bustling about wiping down tables, and we have the opportunity for more than the normal gratuitous conversation we have at the coffee counter. Turns out, she is a writer as well...hooray: a like-minded soul!! She begins to tell me about some writer's conferences that are new to me, and we excitedly talk about writing and books. We plan to get together to write, brainstorm, critique and chat.

A connection has been made...whether it turns into a friendship or a working relationship or nothing...we had today. Our conversations in the future will always have elements of writing and books. We will most certainly learn from each other honoring the threads that connect us.

Serendipity, as explained by the author, Peter H. Reynolds is a perfect description and visualization of this phenomenon. He says, "Serendipity is putting a quarter in the gumball machine and having three pieces come out instead of one-all red."

Wishing you an interesting journey, and many three red gumball kind of days!!

THE SINGING ROAD

AMERICA IS A BEAUTIFUL COUNTRY, there is so much natural beauty to see. This country of ours has mountains and valleys, streams, rivers, and oceans, prairies and canyons, glaciers and swamps. I have traveled to most of the 50 states and hope to see all of them someday. I have to admit, a few of the states I claim have been drive-throughs, but technically I have been in those states!

There are places that are very well known because they are so majestic and awe-inspiring. In addition, there are some fun places to go that are little known. One of those places I would like to tell you about is a place on historic Route 66.

A few years ago the New Mexico Department of Transportation and the National Geographic Channel had an idea to jazz up a stretch of this highway that was somewhat unremarkable. The area is near Tijeras, New Mexico, population 541, twelve miles from Albuquerque.

Their idea was to create a stretch of highway that would "sing" to the drivers passing over it. The idea became reality. Extreme engineering and musicality had to work together to make the "notes" actually play. I love it when imagination turns into reality. They installed rumble strips that would play the song "America the Beautiful," if the drivers drove over the strips at exactly 45 miles per hour. No speeding here if you want to experience this! I have not been here, but it is high on my list!!

Finding these hidden gems when I research an area to travel to is very rewarding. Some of the neatest experiences are small ones. Soak up every sight, sound, and experience you can, wherever you are.

Here are a few lesser-known places to check out if you are in the area, or make a point to be in the area!!

- Paper House in Rockport, Massachusetts (North of Boston) A house and furniture made from 100,000 pieces of newspaper
- Apostle Islands National Lakeshore, Wisconsin
- Devil's Tower, Wyoming

- Seaside, Oregon
- World's Largest Ball of Paint, Indiana
- Guernsey Rut, Guernsey, Wyoming (1 of 9 places where the wheel tracks from those traveling the Oregon Trail can still be seen,)
- Madison Boulder, Madison, New Hampshire

Enjoy all your travels whether they be to places large or small, near or far, betwixt or between! Ibn Battutg said, "Traveling-it leaves you speechless, then turns you into a storyteller."

UKULELE LESSONS

IN MY ENDLESS quest for new learning opportunities and adventures, I am now the proud owner of a concert ukulele and taking lessons. I can't take the whole credit for attempting this. My dear friend Debby had learn to play the ukulele on her bucket list, and of course, wanted a partner in crime. I am always happy to oblige my friends...unless they are moving or cleaning their house. Otherwise, I am available.

It seems that the first step in playing the ukulele is obtaining a ukulele to play. So off we went to our beloved local music store, West Music.

A very nice gentleman, Chris, who was not normally on the sales floor was summoned to assist us. He may have been from security, I'm not sure. He happily humored us and joined in our shenanigans while we tried out ukuleles. We each picked out a beautiful ukulele, music book, and tuner. I shared with him the fact that if indeed we learned to play and thereafter went on the road that we were ready with a name for our act: The Uku-Ladies. He was duly impressed and made us promise to autograph our first CD for him.

We made our purchases and Chris set us up for back to back lessons once a week. The adventure of purchasing the ukes was so much fun, we almost didn't need to take lessons...of course, then we wouldn't need the ukuleles. Life is complicated.

Stay tuned for more stories as the lessons commence. I have a ukulele and I know how to use it.

Take a chance, try something new. It's good for your brain, your heart, and your soul. Wishing you a somewhere over the rainbow, tiptoeing through the tulips kind of day.

SEEDS OF HAPPINESS

WE HAD A NEW ADVENTURE RECENTLY, what I like to call a field trip. Pure happenstance that I heard about this place which is only about 30 minutes from home.

A beautiful August Saturday in Iowa, with blue skies, sun, and an almost fall-like temperature. Fueled by coffee, cereal and our desire to see something new and different we hit the road. We knew the general area of our destination, but not the exact location. However, since everything on the internet is true, we relied on the website's statement: "You can't miss us." Good enough for me.

Watching eagerly for our destination to appear, we crested a small hill, and there it was, truly in all of its glory!! Three acres of sunflowers, a crop not typically grown in Iowa. I am not sure why that is, as Nebraska, North Dakota and Kansas all grow sunflowers as a cash crop.

It was a stunning sight. We approached from the east, and all the sunflower heads were facing us. "Wow" succinctly describes the sight of all these yellow, happy sunflowers growing in the field. The venue is called Pheasant Run Farm. It is a family farm growing produce, herbs, and flowers for the wholesale market. This was their first year for a sunflower field. They are not raising the sunflowers for market, but planned this as an adventure for families to come, enjoy, be outside and learn something about sunflowers. A single large sunflower can produce 1,000 seeds!! For a small admission fee, you could enjoy walking the field on small paths cleared by the farmer, and cut one sunflower to take home. Additional sunflowers could be cut and paid for if desired.

I was amazed and delighted to walk among these beauties of nature. They were taller than I was, and the heads of the sunflowers were the size of dinner plates! It wasn't until we were leaving and cut ours, that I realized how heavy the heads were. No wonder the stalks are so thick and strong!!

We learned lots about sunflowers during our walk. The largest producer of sunflowers is the state of North Dakota. I would have guessed Kansas, having seen the massive fields of sunflowers there. As the sunflower grows, during the day the head will turn and follow the sun. At night, they return to an east-facing position, maybe in readiness for the morning sun. When the head becomes too heavy as it nears maturity, they can no longer turn, and they will all face east. Of course, being a color outside the lines kind of girl, I wondered if there are any rogue sunflowers that don't follow the rules. I was unable to collect any data concerning that.

I am fascinated by the daily journey of these flowers from east to west. Clearly, they must have some kind of circadian rhythm and sensitivity to light to drive this ritual. I am not interested in researching this for scientific explanations. Some wondrous things are better when we just believe in the miracle of it all.

Maybe, people would thrive more if they followed the lead of the sunflower. Point your face to the sun, the positive things in life, and don't turn to the dark side. Historically, the sunflower stands for adoration, longevity, and loyalty. Just the name of this beautiful plant makes me smile. Sunflower comes from the Greek words "helios" for Sun, and "anthos" for flowers.

Wouldn't Sunflower be a lovely name for a baby girl? It takes me back to the "hippie era" in which I came of age. Bring on the bell-bottom jeans, peace, love and rock 'n roll! Maybe we can create a whole new baby boom with "hippie" names!! Bring on Moonbeam, Serenity Winter, Arlo, Dylan, Lavender, Harmony, and Aquarius. That would be a very fun class list for the teacher.

Pardon my digression, as I slipped back in time! Back to the sunflowers that inspired this writing...I smiled the entire time we were there. Being among these beautiful living flowers was calming, breathtaking and peaceful. It was a place to reap the seeds of happiness. We will definitely return next year!

Of course, a road trip wouldn't be complete without lunch in a local diner. We wandered into Belle Plaine and ate at the somewhat famous Lincoln Cafe. This is where the story takes a dark turn...We ordered a SECOND breakfast, and couldn't pass up the homemade pie. The breakfast servings turned out to be super-sized, so we did have to take the raspberry and peach pie slices home with us to eat later.

Seek out adventures, road trips, sights, and sounds whenever you can. You never know what you might find or experience, and it can turn into a memory you will treasure. Brooke Hampton, Author said this: "I hope there are days when your coffee tastes like magic, your playlist makes you dance, strangers make you smile, and the night sky touches your soul. I hope there are days when you fall in love with being alive.."

This was one of those days. Wishing you love, laughter, adventures and raspberry pie for the rest of your days.

DOGGIE BAG

IT ALL BEGAN with a road trip to Huntsville, Texas for high school graduation for one of my nine bonus grandchildren. I spent a week in

Dallas many years ago, but didn't truly experience the "real" Texas. After all, as their tourism ads used to proclaim, it's a "whole other country." I was attending a national banking school and didn't see much other than the campus of Southern Methodist University.

So as we began the trip, I am anticipating seeing the "real" Texas. The beginning of the trip was unusual. There had been tornadoes in Missouri and Oklahoma the night before, and we needed to alter our travel route because of closed roads, no power and general chaos in some damaged areas. The trip was fairly non-eventful, albeit very long. I am a don't fence me in kinda gal, and small confined spaces make me restless and uncomfortable.

I managed to keep myself entertained, and began to daydream about lunch. It's the little things that help the time to pass!! First food in the "real" Texas...has to be Mexican or barbeque..let the quest begin. My beau, who has made this journey many times was sure he knew a little town that had numerous barbecue options. Let's do this!! We exited the interstate and spent fifteen minutes or more driving around a ramshackle kind of town with no results, hence no lunch. Gave up, and got back on the interstate, and lo and behold, this town had a second exit. We have hit the big time now!! It certainly wasn't "bright lights, big city," but we had hope. Driving...driving...driving...no barbeque...very few restaurants. We surrendered. It was well past lunchtime according to my very accurate and demanding digestive system. There will be plenty of other times to experience Texas food. Let's just eat!

So what to our wondering eyes should appear, but a familiar sight...wait for it...yes, it's Panda Express. Really? This is the best we can do? Nothing against their food, I am a fan of Panda Express, just did not seem appropriate that our first meal in Texas would be from a "Fast Casual Chinese

Restaurant." We ordered, enjoying the break from the car and some good food.

As a writer, I am an inveterate people watcher. Public places provide hours of interesting slices of life. As we are finishing, I see a couple buying lots of different ala carte items. As I continue to watch, I see they have five children with them. They are attempting to purchase food, find seats, corral all the children and have some lunch. It was almost as entertaining as a circus. As we prepared to exit, our path took us near them. As I passed by, I thought I heard a dog bark , Weird. Then I hear it again. I take a closer look and yes, there is a dog, in a mesh carrier kind of bag. I hoped it wasn't a "hot"dog, in any sense of the meaning!

I could barely get to the car before I started laughing. All I could think to say to Verne, (the aforementioned beau) between giggles was:

'They have five kids and a dog in a bag." Even typing the words is making me laugh again.

Take a look around you, watch people living their lives, and think about how you are living yours. Smiles, laughter, Panda Express...life is good.

TABLE IT

I FEEL I must recognize Cassie, a woman who has changed my life, saved my life and puts up with my craziness. She is my massage therapist and has worked wonders on this tired, somewhat old body of mine. I made a decision to see her regularly as it seems I am reaping some health benefits from these visits.

She has helped me heal and reduced my pain after a car accident, a gravity storm that produced a couple of cracked ribs, and life in general. I will have to say it has been a learning experience for me, and probably for her too. One she didn't ask for! She is truly a muscle whisperer and fixes problems I didn't know I had.

She was working on my legs, and said, "Wow, that's really tight." I am puffing up, feeling good about myself, after all, when you are old, you want things to be tight. Well, evidently having tight calf muscles that are constantly in knots isn't something for me to take pride in. I do have to mention, however, I have never fallen off the massage table.

On my last visit, while entertaining a monster cold, she did wonders on my face and sinuses. I was kind of a rock star that day as well if I do say so myself. I threw a tissue across the room and hit the wastebasket...left-handed...lying on my stomach...without my glasses on...in a darkened room. Cassie tried not to show it, but she was pretty impressed, who wouldn't be?

If you have never visited a massage therapist, I highly recommend it for your well-being. There are 744 hours in a month, surely you can spare one to take care of yourself with a healing massage.

CENTRAL PARK VIEW

NEW YORK CITY is my would've, could've, and should've alternate fantasy life. There are many opportunities I should have considered when I was young, brave, free and had no obligations to tie me to a particular place. Looking back, New York City would have been my destination. I think I could have thrived in the city that never sleeps. Living, working, exploring all the niches, nooks and crannies of the big city sounds like a dream.

I have always loved all things NYC, but only in recent years had the chance to spend a week there. My illusions were not shattered, in fact, quite the opposite. As we walked through the neighborhoods, I could picture myself popping out of one of the brownstones, ready to step into whatever the day had to offer. But alas, that dream is not to come true unless I win the lottery (which I rarely play) and can afford to buy a pied-a-terre in the "city."

The polar opposite of a bustling New York City neighborhood is the amazing 840-acre green space in the middle of Manhattan: Central Park. It is stunning in the spring, and I imagine it is also a thing of beauty in the other seasons. I wonder, (I know, here we go again.) what would a statue in Central Park experience in all the seasons if it had human sensory abilities? (Who wouldn't wonder about this?)

A statue's view of the seasons…

Spring…ahh the beauty of this time of year. This green space I live in is showing off too many shades of green to count…emerald, lime, peridot, pickle, fern, chartreuse, (for years I thought chartreuse was a shade of purple or magenta…) olive, sage, well you get the idea!! When they mow the grass it smells like heaven. The abundant flower beds are blooming and a cacophony of color for the eyes. Unfortunately,

spring seems to bring a population explosion of pigeons…need I say more? Thank goodness for spring rain showers!

Summer...people are everywhere!! I love to watch them picnic, stroll on the walking paths, throw a frisbee and lay on the grass and dream the day away. I especially like to watch the people try to row the boats. Lots of them don't know how to do it and end up rowing in circles or running into other people in boats. I probably shouldn't laugh, but they provide me hours of entertainment! More people here than any other time of year, I think. When people stop to visit Strawberry Fields, with the Imagine memorial to John Lennon, I remember so vividly the day he was shot across the street at the Dakota apartment building. I always thought that building was spooky looking anyway. "Imagine" what he might have done had his life not been taken that way? So much more music we would have had.

Autumn...in New York...love that song and love the season. It is my favorite season here in my beloved spot in Central Park. The crowds of people are diminishing, so it's a bit quieter. Our thousands of trees are dressed in their best-colored finery for the season. There isn't a red carpet dress that can match their fiery reds and oranges that change with the light. They put on a show that is unmatchable! As the leaves float slowly to the ground, they become a crunchy, crispy carpet for the visitors to walk on.

Winter...I do enjoy the snowfall blanketing the park around me. It muffles the sounds and makes this a quiet wonderland. I adore watching the lovers walking hand in hand as the snowflakes covered their coats and hats. I feel sorry for the frequent dog walkers as they must brave not only the nice winter days, but the bitter ones as well to pick up, well, you know...Those dogs are almost as bad as the pigeons. The air smells fresh and the crispness of the cold renews my energy.

The ice skaters are full of energy and it is fun to watch their colorful coats and stocking hats twirl around on the ice. I promise I don't laugh (much) when their derriere meets the ice.

I hope you have enjoyed seeing a little bit of the park through the eyes of my statue!! Robert Benchley, American humorist and newspaper columnist said this: "Central Park is the grandiose symbol of the front yard that each child in New York hasn't got." Funny, but true. Thank goodness, they have this marvelous place to go and enjoy all that nature has to offer them.

New York, New York something for everyone! I plan to continue my love affair with this city and hope to visit again soon.

GLAMOUR PHOTO

I WANTED to share with you today an experience I recently had. I am guessing you have seen advertisements for having your photograph done by a professional in a glamour shoot. The models in the ads are dressed in glamorous, sexy clothes in a soft, filtered background. You might not even recognize your own mother in one of these photos. They do an amazing job, but this is not an inexpensive proposition.

While researching this, I found a much more frugal option.

There is a place called the Driver's License Station, where they will take your picture at a much lower cost. The only requirement is to get a new driver's license. They don't provide costumes or special lighting so you will need to arrive dressed in the clothing in which you would like to have your picture taken. Not everyone takes advantage of this, so don't be surprised if other clients are not as dressed up as you are.

Preparation for the actual photo is easy: take off your glasses, get your hair out of your eyes, open your eyes wide and smile with your mouth closed. Before you even know it, the photo is done. I was quite pleased with my most recent photo. Of course, in the last one, I looked like I had just been rescued after a near drowning in a muddy pond.

Improvement was easy to come by, so the photographer/employee doesn't get all the credit for my new glamour driver's license photo.

Do be aware that you will not be allowed to take or use a selfie for this particular photo, and they don't allow the use of props. Fun-haters.

Hoping this has been helpful, just out here doing what I can to add some silliness to your life. Milton Berle, legendary actor and comedian said, "Laughter is an instant vacation." Don't wait, take one today!!

HAIRDO OR DON'T?

I SHOULD START out by saying, I don't think "hairdo" is really a term in common usage anymore. It reminds me of a bygone era, maybe the 1950s, when women got their hair "done." Now we might say styled, or cut or "blown out." I am writing about this for several reasons. My long-time hair-stylist/friend/honorary family member had demanded her own page in this book as she feels she was overlooked in my first book. Well, when someone you allow to stand behind you with scissors close to your head demands something, a smart person would comply.

The whole crux of our relationship is about power. I have none. Stephanie decides what my hair is going to look like: cut, color, style, it is all about her. My only power is allowing her to continue to be my stylist. Although, I am pretty sure if I didn't schedule an appointment she would hunt me down and cut my hair on the spot. She is a force to be reckoned with. A testament to her power is that I am still with her, after the eventful visit when she said, "I don't like your hair." If asked, she will say I didn't let her finish the sentence, but I think what she said was pretty clear.

Joking aside, I love Stephanie and she takes the trials and tribulations I have with my hair seriously and does a great job making me look as good as possible, considering what she has to work with. In addition, we have laughed and cried together over the years over deaths, births, accidents, and life in general. She is an important person in the circle of women with whom I surround myself.

“If your hair is done properly and you have on good shoes, you can get away with anything.”

— IRIS APFEL, AMERICAN FASHION ICON

So thanks, Stephanie for arming me properly for my many misadventures and accompanying me on some of them!!

BLOOM WHERE YOU ARE PLANTED

THIS SPRING and summer have provided us with some unusual weather patterns here in the Heartland (and indeed across the country). It rained, rained, rained, and then it rained some more. Many farmers were late getting their crops in the ground because it was always raining, or a muddy swamp. Finally, the crops get planted, and driving through the countryside I can see the unusual variance in the height of the corn on different farms. After the crops were in, we had days of extreme heat and humidity. Day after day after day, with no relief.

Now the crops are begging for rain!!

One particular crop has flourished with this weather. A vivid splotch of tangerine thrives against the many shades of green in the Iowa country-side. Commonly known as ditch lilies, a type of daylily, there is a proliferation of these flowers this summer. The ditches are full of these wonderfully vibrant volunteer flowers!! These flowers bloom for 30-40 days, sharing their beauty! They appear almost magically and color our ditches for the summer. I have enjoyed seeing them so much this year, after the weather vagaries that tormented the farmers, and indeed all Iowans.

We don't always get to choose where we are planted, but we can be like the ditch lily and bloom, grow, survive, thrive and share our blossoms and beauty with the world.

❤ ❤ ❤

MY UKULELE SET MIX

I HAVE LEARNED many lessons in my life, but none as fun as my current undertaking...wait for it...I am playing the ukulele. As I write this, I have had eighteen half-hour lessons, and I look forward to each one.

My teacher, Dan, is a tall, gentle giant of a man with a mop of dark curly hair. He takes everything I do or say in stride, which not everyone is up for!! In my first lesson, I walked in, and said as a way of introducing myself said, "I have never played a musical instrument, never learned to read music, I am old and probably not teachable."

His only comment was, " I am older than you, I think." Well, he is not, by a long shot, older than me. Points for gentleman Dan!! He is patient, and not critical of my musical faux pas and general lack of understanding of many things musical.

After eighteen lessons, I can read music like a pro. I have graduated from my beginner songs of "Eensy Weensy Spider," "Freres Jacques," and learning scales. I quickly mastered (?) those ditties and moved on.

Slowly, week by week, Dan adds songs, one or two a week to what he calls my "set mix." That cracks me up every time. I will not be playing any gigs with my beloved uke, of that I am sure!! I do love having a set mix, however!! Sometimes two new songs is a stretch for this newbie musical student!

My set mix currently includes some Elvis tunes (of course), Beatles, "Edelweiss," the "Iowa Fight Song", the "Star-Spangled Banner", "Happy Birthday", "Somewhere Over the Rainbow," (I think there may be a law that if you play the ukulele, you have to learn this song), and a number of others. Every week, I excitedly anticipate what song Dan might add to my set mix. (I never get tired of saying that!)

I had always wanted to play the acoustic guitar, fooled around a bit with one on my own, but I think you can guess how far that went. The ukulele is smaller and easier to handle, easier to reach the notes and very portable.

If you have never played a musical instrument, now is the time!! It is so very satisfying to learn a new skill and force your brain to learn and act in a different way. The first time I played a song through, and it was totally recognizable was thrilling!!

I love trying new things, adding experiences to my repertoire and learning! (I am kind of a nerd, I like it when I have homework!)

As someone great, but unknown once said, "It's hard to frown when ukulele music is goin' down!"

Add something to your set mix on a regular basis, your life will be ever changed for the better and your brain will thank you. Claude Debussy, French composer said, "Music is the arithmetic of sounds, as optics is the geometry of light." Let's do some.

SORRY, WE HAVE NO TOADS

I HAD the enlightening experience of selling my first book at a local Artists and Crafts event. As is normal for me and others, when business was slow, the vendors got a little crazy. Well, at least my friends and I might have...allegedly...there is no proof...

I made friends with the owners of the booth across from us over the three days. It was slow towards the end of one day, approaching the seven o'clock hour and traffic was infrequent. My new friends wanted to go into the casino where the event was being held and try their luck at a little gambling. They asked me to watch their booth as well as my own. I was all over that.

I don't know where the trouble began. As the time neared for them to return, someone thought it would be funny if I crawled under their table and scared them when they came back. We all agreed it would be hilarious. I am the oldest of the group that was there, clearly not the wisest, and the last one that should be crawling under a table. At least if I am already on the floor, I can't have a gravity storm. There is that.

So as I prepared to accomplish this we realized that under the front table, there was no space for me as it was filled with supplies. They had a large booth, so the next idea was to get under the side or back tables. I lifted the draping covering one of the side tables, and it too was stuffed. I looked across the aisle, as a father and young son walked by and proclaimed to my friends, " I can't fit under there, it is full of totes." The young boy stopped, his face alight, and asked, "Are there toads under there?" I am sure he was thinking, maybe this whole day won't be a total waste if they have toads. I invited him to look under the table and replied, "No, there are totes, plastic boxes under the table."

His face fell, the light went out of his eyes and I would have given anything to have a toad to give or show him. I had dashed his dreams. A few simple words and his hope for a break from his boredom was crushed. I could think of nothing more to say to him that could make things better.

They moved on, and he gave one more backward glance over his shoulder to make sure I wasn't getting toads out of there.

I hesitate to tell you the end of the story, but I feel I must. My friends and I might have been a little punchy at the end of our long day of bookselling. After he was out of sight, we were hysterical with laughter, maybe even to the point of tears. Even now, one of us can randomly say, "Are there toads under there?" and we will break into laughter.

I may have dashed his dreams for the day, but that little boy sure gave three mature (well, that might be a stretch) women a whole big bunch of laughter. I hope he finds his toads someday, and as his world gets larger and his dreams get bigger, I hope he finds those too.

Walt Disney (visionary and dream creator) said, "All our dreams can come true. If we have the courage to pursue them."

FAQs FROM THE SIXTH GRADE

IT HAS BEEN my pleasure (mostly) to have been a guest teacher at a middle school for the last thirteen years. I enjoy the ages and the differences between 6th, 7th and 8th-graders. The independence, maturity, and problem-solving skills that emerge during this time period are fascinating to watch.

Each age level has its own special ways of entertaining and amusing the teachers, but I think the sixth-graders might win the prize for the most creative remarks and actions.

Questions I have been asked by sixth-grade students:

- How old are you?
- Can I see your driver's license?
- Is this a full-time job?
- Why don't you just get your own classroom?
- Do you believe in God?
- Did you dye your hair? Was it a prank?
- Am I your favorite student?
- What do you do when you aren't here?
- Do you have a husband?
- Do you get paid for this?
- Can I touch your ring (necklace, watch, iPad, whatever!)?
- What games do you have on your phone?

These kids are funny, curious, kind, and caring but not above trying to get away with a little something when the "real" teacher is absent!! As we often say, you can't scare me, I teach middle school.

" "Teaching middle school is an adventure, not a job."

— ANGELA K. BENNETT, AUTHOR

♥ ♥ ♥

A CASE FOR LOVE

SOME YEARS AGO, my twin sister from another mother had an idea for a project. I should preface this by saying, whenever one of us gets an idea, the other one is expected to join in without question and with all the enthusiasm she can muster. This has led to many enjoyable adventures, some "what happens in Vegas" types of adventures, and some very fulfilling adventures. This story is about one of the latter.

Sue's idea was to start a grassroots project, where we could see the results of our labors touch a local not-for-profit organization and their clients. We decided to make pillowcases. I can hear you out there, thinking, not such a big deal. I think you are wrong, it was a big deal.

The project was to make pillowcases for every guest at the local Domestic Violence shelter. We sought the help of the bank we both worked for, and they agreed to purchase new pillows. We enlisted the help of many friends who were quilters or seamstresses. Our thought was to give every resident a new pillow and pillowcase that they could take with them when they left. Many of the residents arrive with nothing, so we would provide something personal that would be theirs when they left to go to a more permanent home.

We chose sports teams, superheroes, princesses, dinosaurs, trucks and a myriad of other fabric choices that would appeal to children. For the mothers, we chose fabrics that were fun, beautiful, feminine, inspirational, something for every taste. We hoped that knowing a pillowcase was made for them personally would let them know someone cared. We called our little project "A Case for Love."

For one year, we provided the shelter with pillows and pillowcases for all their residents. The final count was 600. That's a lot of love. We never met any of these people, but hope that the positive energy, love, and care that went into the making of this simple project touched them in some way.

If I were doing this again, I think I would add a flashlight complete with batteries for the children. Life is very hard sometimes, and something to light the dark night is a very good thing. Eleanor Roosevelt, Former First Lady said, "It is better to light a candle than to curse the darkness." On your journey, be the light in the darkness for others and the light will shine even brighter on your path.

BEWARE THE COFFEE PODS

I LOVE A GOOD ROAD TRIP. The siren song of the highway, the sights to see along the way, and scintillating conversation for hours upon end. Road trips usually involve overnight stays on the way to our destination. Hotels have evolved since the days of yore, and offer many "perks" to travelers seeking shelter and rest from their day's journey.

One of these "perks" is coffee makers in the hotel room. That is a great idea...no wandering down to the lobby in your pajamas in the wee small hours of the morning to find that first cup of coffee. (Not that I have ever done that...much...) Ahhh..the magic, the anticipation, and then reality smacks me not so gently as I see the dreaded coffee pods.

They seem harmless and convenient. I am lulled into a sense of security in my early morning fogginess, as I approach the tiny coffee maker. Seems simple enough...add water, insert the disposable holder with a paper packet of coffee inside, then plug the machine in.

Do not, I repeat, do not plug it in until the coffee is inserted and a coffee cup is in place or you will have hot water all over everything in the vicinity. Don't ask me how I know this.

Okay, so I've done everything correctly, and a brown substance is coming from the coffee maker into my cup. Can it be true? Is this coffee? Sorry to have to say, but in most cases, not really. My experience has been it is bitter, brown water that bears little resemblance to coffee's aroma or taste. At my last stay, I dumped all the packages of creamers and sweeteners into the cup trying to create something drinkable, it couldn't be done. How hard can it be to put real coffee in those packets? Another of life's unanswerable questions!! Wishing you real coffee to start the day and endless blessings along the way.

INTERESTING SOCKS ...

SOME YEARS AGO, I arrived at my doctor's office for my annual "female" exam. I start with this in case some of you want to stop reading right here! The medical assistant entered and did all of the preliminary checks of my vital signs: blood pressure, temperature, weight, cocktail preference...oops...that's a different story. Everything was fine. She then proceeded to give me the standard instructions: Take everything off, and here is a paper towel to cover yourself with until the doctor comes in. To be perfectly honest, it wasn't really a paper towel, it was much thinner than my paper towels at home. It was a "robe" made of transparent, thin paper. Ahh...the fashion statement.

After giving me the instructions, she exited the room and gave me privacy to undress and use the paper towel. I complied, being the rule follower that I am, with one exception. I left my socks on because my feet get cold, and I was pretty sure she wasn't going to be looking there.

The doctor enters, we exchange pleasantries and then I lie back on the exam table. My feet go in the stirrups, (no gentleman, there is no horse here) and the exam begins. As she is finishing up, she says, "Huh, interesting socks." I thought that was kind of weird. As those of you who read my first book know, I am a fancy, colorful sock kind of gal. I appreciate the compliment on my taste in socks but still thought it strange.

She leaves the exam room, and I promptly discard the paper towel and begin to dress. As I am putting on my shoes, I notice my socks and realize they don't match, really, at all. I do wear mismatched socks on occasion, but it is usually to entertain the students at the Middle School where I am a guest teacher. I don't usually do that for interaction with the regular public or for appointments.

My first thought was "Whew, now I understand the sock comment." I don't know what my doctor thought. I had been a patient for a number of years, and she knew I don't always color inside the lines. It is now probably a comment in my medical file, which will be used someday to explain any strange behavior I might exhibit.

Life is short if you have better things to do, eat dessert, learn to play the harmonica and don't sort the socks.

BOOK CLUB ADVENTURE

PUBLISHING my first book sent me on many adventures that I never expected. They were all delightful in different ways. The most recent adventure occurred when a long-time friend, Fran, told me her book club chose my book ("Mama Said There'd Be Days Like This") for their book of the month. Since it is a book with daily readings, they were reading one page a day. Although, as always, there were some rule-breakers who read the whole thing! I identify with these rule-breakers!! They invited me to come to their meeting and talk about my book. Score!! I love talking (surprise!) and I love talking about my book!! Touchdown and extra point!!

Fran lives in a somewhat rural area, on a long and winding road...It was dark. I entered her address in my Google Maps on my phone for moral support and help to find her house. It had been some years since I had been there, added to the fact that I am directionally challenged. That's a real thing. I have directional dyslexia. Anyway, that's my excuse. I knew I was getting close as I rounded a curve. I am not in front of or near a house, and Google Maps suddenly announced, "You have arrived!" I must confess my first thought was, well, I did publish a book, I am kind of famous. Then I realized the next house was hers, and Google was announcing my destination. Another balloon burst, but there was the split-second of pure joy before reality reared up and slapped me in the face.

I did not know any of the club members except Fran, our hostess. It did not take very long and I felt like I was one of the group. Eight women who welcomed me. They were funny, articulate, loved to read and they all had stories. As a bonus, there was pizza, wine, beer, and cookies. It has been a long time since I met a group of women I liked so much instantly. We laughed, talked, laughed, and enjoyed adult beverages. Did I mention we laughed?

I will never forget that night or those women. Another group of women who decorated my life. They promised to invite me again. I am looking forward to that next time, whenever it happens. I am thankful that they welcomed me, made me feel valued and shared parts of their life with me.

Eleanor Roosevelt said, "Many people will walk in and out of your life, but only true friends will leave footprints on your heart." Treasure those friends. Find your tribe, your group, your girl squad. There is nothing more powerful than a group of women sharing their thoughts and their lives. May you be blessed with true and loyal friends by your side as you walk through life. Your journey of thousands of days will be better for it.

BRADLEY

ONE OF THE things I enjoy about traveling, is the people you meet and the things they teach you about life. You never know when you are going to have an interaction with someone who changes your life, and who you will never forget. In case you haven't noticed, people are everywhere.

We were shopping in a Kroger grocery store, getting huge amounts of water, wine, snacks and what-have-you to replenish supplies at the lake house where our family had gathered. It was a lengthy adventure, as it always is in an unfamiliar grocery store. Adding to the length of the adventure, were the very specific requests from certain family members. (It's okay, we still love you.)

Ahoy, at last, the checkout counter is in sight and we can find our way out of the store. As Verne unloads the cart, I move to the end of the checkout, as I like to pack the groceries or help if I can. This is when I met my new friend, Bradley. Bradley was a differently-abled person who was eager to pack our groceries and place them back in the cart.

I was wearing one of my many "Iowa" shirts as I like to do when we travel. They are definitely conversation starters and a way to find all the amazing connections that despite differences and geography, it really is a small world! Bradley looked at my shirt, and asked me, "Are you from Iowa?" I answered in the affirmative. His face lit up and he said three simple words: "Field of Dreams." I told him we didn't live too far from the Field of Dreams movie site. He said, "That is the best movie ever." I agreed. We continued to talk as he peppered me with questions about Iowa, about how I got to Texas from Iowa. He also wanted to make sure I still lived in Iowa and was just visiting. It was probably a ten-minute conversation and could have gone on longer.

I think he would have followed me out of the store to continue chatting if he wasn't such a hard worker and dedicated to doing his job.

I smiled all the way on our drive back to the lake, and the rest of the day. I am smiling now as I remember Bradley. He was very special, and once again, an Iowa connection because of my t-shirt and an iconic movie. Bradley, if I could grant you a wish, it would be that you could visit the Field of Dreams someday. Keep working hard, keep watching that movie and may all your dreams come true.

THE "EYES" HAVE IT

As I wrote in an earlier story in this book, I have spent a fair amount of time at the eye clinic at University of Iowa Hospitals and Clinics.

After my last surgery it was time for the month after post-op check, I am ushered into the exam room, and wait patiently for my surgeon. Because the University of Iowa Hospitals and Clinics is a teaching hospital, one must expect that sometimes a "student" will see you first. (Did I mention it has one of the best ophthalmology departments in the world?)

I sit patiently in the chair, looking around to see if there are any gadgets I could try out and not get caught. A woman enters the room, wearing a white coat and a badge that proclaims she is a doctor. I do like the custom at this hospital, that every provider wears a badge with their position on it. Nice to know who is helping, and who you are talking to.

This doctor is a "fellow" in the eye clinic. A fellow is someone who has completed medical school and residency and can practice medicine. The fellow title enters in because they are getting additional training in a specialty, such as ophthalmology. So, Dr. "Fellow" starts the exam, putting my eyes through the customary paces. She has to continually tell me to look straight ahead because my eyes are wandering.

What appears to my wandering eye is a necklace, unlike anything I have seen. It is an almond-shaped pendant, with a black stone in the middle. Framing the top of the pendant is a series of tiny diamonds. Are you with me? This necklace looks exactly like an eye, suspended on a gold chain. I can't take "my" eyes off of it. Hence the admonitions from her, to keep looking straight ahead.

It really was a lovely piece, if you didn't look too closely. I do hope this isn't a new fad among doctors. I am sure that I do not want to see certain parts of the human anatomy dangling on chains from my doctor's neck. Nephrologists, Brain Surgeons, Urologists, and Podiatrists come quickly to mind.

I am grateful for the amazing doctors that take care of my eyes. The world is a beautiful place, and I am happy to keep seeing it. Be thankful for your eyes, schedule your annual checkups, and as comedian Norm Crosby advises us, "If your eyes hurt after you drink coffee, you have to take the spoon out of the cup."

TALES OF A BOOKSELLER

As I work on crafting this book of stories, my first book has been for sale for about 5 months. There are no words for the excitement, fulfillment and even disbelief as "Mama Said There'd Be Days Like This," has been on sale for all the world to see.

I have loved doing the book talks, meeting people and seeing them buy my books. I love getting a call from one of the stores where it is sold telling me they need more inventory. I love seeing the sales reports from Amazon each month. I love having my dream come true…

I am pretty sure you are waiting for the other shoe to drop, so here it is. I decided to try an experiment and applied to be part of an Arts and Crafts Fair, a three-day event at a local casino. I was aware that the attendees would not be there to find a book. They are looking for unique gifts, home decor, and tchotchkes. It could be a tough venture, and the giving up of three days of my life and my friends who offered to help with the booth!

I quickly discovered, the only way to sell my book in this venue was to talk to people as they walked by and tell them about my book. Some might call it accosting innocent, unaware customers. I tried different sales spiels as I would get tired of repeating the same words. I am a pretty good sales-person, after all, I was the top cookie seller in my Girl Scout Troop in 6th grade. My greatest accomplishment at this event was when I sold 5 books to people who told me they don't read…yep, send me to the Sahara to sell sand, I am all over it.

I probably talked to 200 people individually and gave my sales pitch.

That is mentally and physically exhausting, to pitch books to people who aren't looking to buy books. It's a good thing I take rejection well. I did sell quite a few books, but I had to work for every single one. But, boy howdy, did I get some stories out of this!! Let me share one...

Possibly the most interesting and simultaneously creepy and scary event happened when I was away from the booth. I was returning from a break, and a man walked up to me, and said, "Are you the author?" My first reaction was one of delight that a "fan" recognized me. Move over James Patterson, David Baldacci and Fern Michaels, I am joining your club. When I replied in the affirmative, that I was the author, everything went south. He started "speaking," but to me, it was just sounds, no words and it went on for a few minutes. I didn't know what to do. It crossed my mind that one of us might be having a stroke. I just stood there, frozen. Eventually, he said, "You must not speak Czech." I mean, I know that's unusual in Iowa to come across someone who doesn't speak Czech. The explanation was that he noticed my surname, and recognized it as Czech. Still, a pretty big leap to randomly start speaking Czech to someone you don't know. I married into that name, and I do know that my late husband, his parents, and grandparents did not speak Czech. I am a writer and I do know many words, but the majority of them are in English!

Despite the challenges of this event, there was some treasure to be discovered. As I mentioned being a Girl Scout earlier, a song we used to sing came to mind.

"Make new friends, but keep the old,
One is silver and the other gold."

We sang this song often, sometimes together, sometimes as a "round." The truth of these simple words is timeless, and I feel like it was very applicable to my weekend bookselling adventure.

My "old" friends supported me, encouraging me to apply to be part of the event, promising their help. One traveled two hours to be here, she and others gave up their weekend to help me succeed. Their friendship is a treasure beyond any value that could be placed upon it.

The new friends I made were helpful, funny, ready to participate in my silliness and had big hearts. It seemed immediately as if we knew each other forever. We spent three days together, and I am certain we will make an effort to cross paths and have another adventure. I am a collector of many things, but my most prized collection consists of the people that I meet and keep in my life and my heart.

I believe we don't meet people by accident. We meet them for a reason, for a lesson, for a chance to make a change in our life, and to find hearts that speak to ours. Meeting someone new is opening a new door to a new world. Take chances, open doors and open your minds and hearts to new possibilities.

> "So I say to you: Ask and it will be given to you; seek and you will find; knock and the door will be opened to you."

— Luke 11:9 NIV

NO ID, NO PROBLEM

I LOVE HAVING NEW ADVENTURES, attending movies, musical concerts, talks, learning to throw a tomahawk...you get the idea. I became aware that former First Lady, Laura Bush, was going to speak as part of a lecture series, in a venue near us. It was a ninety-minute drive and came with the added bonus of the opportunity to have a quick dinner with my grand-daughter Allison who is a senior at the University of Northern Iowa, where the event was occurring. I ordered the tickets by phone, to be picked up at the Will Call window the evening of the event.

The date arrived, and we began our mini-road trip to the north. It was approximately forty-five minutes into the drive that I realized that I may have not been as prepared for this as common sense would dictate. I did not have my phone, my wallet, or any identification. The phone contained the directions to my granddaughter's house which I needed because I am directionally challenged, even though I had been there before. The phone would have provided the ability to call my granddaughter and obtain directions. However, sometimes all the lucky pennies one has picked up pays dividends.

I discovered that my very new Apple watch has the ability to call people even without having my phone nearby. Woo-double-hoo!! So, obstacle number one is overcome. With this victory under our belts, we decided to pick up our tickets before dinner. Arriving at the venue, we see all kinds of people outside, directing, stopping, searching the approaching guests. Signs tell us that there is heightened security at this event because of the speaker. Bags will be searched. No problem there, I forgot to bring anything.

While my companion (Disclosure: while reading this, he expressed his dislike for the term companion, something to do with a dog...he prefers "main squeeze") Verne, waits in the car, as he wants nothing to do with the potential fiasco of me trying to pick up our tickets with no identification to see a former First Lady...What could possibly go wrong?

I approach the Will Call window courageously, certain that I am going to see Laura Bush speak, no matter what. I am getting in. The young woman at the ticket booth asked my name, and found my tickets. As she was preparing to hand them to me (goal line in sight, friends!) she asks, "Do you have any identification?"

I proceed to explain the unfortunate situation I have placed myself in, and why I don't have any identification. I then say, "I do have a business card." I show it to her and she gives me the tickets. Touchdown and extra point!! Granted, she was a college student, but I have talked myself into and out of situations more dire than this. Those stories will have to wait for another time...if ever!

Happy ending, we enjoyed Mrs. Bush's speech very much and the question and answer session that followed. She is a classy, articulate, self-deprecating and funny woman. It was very much worth the effort to attend.

In conclusion, I might share this advice: Bring your identification, your phone, ibuprofen for the headaches that may occur, and never give up. It never hurts to try!!

PLANTING AN INDOOR GARDEN

THIS YEAR'S birthday was a milestone year, in many ways, including the slightly large number attached to it. As I may have said before, I do not consider myself old, but chronologically gifted. I decided to treat myself this year and do something that I have always wanted to do, but for one reason or another, I never made it happen.

On the morning of my birthday, I headed out to one of my offices, also known as the cafe at Barnes and Noble. On my way, I stopped at the florist and purchased a large bouquet of carnations in a riot of colors. I arrived at the "office," purchased my coffee and settled in to write.

After the store got busier, I began to look for people to surprise with a flower. I began to stroll around and offer flowers to people, telling them it was my birthday gift to do this. The reactions of the recipients was indeed a gift to me.

The first flower I gave to a young woman, who said, "Just seeing the bouquet of flowers gives me joy." I handed her a flower that matched her coat. She smiled and said, "You are going to leave here with more joy than you came in with!" She was so right!!

Each gift of a flower to a stranger elicited smiles, and sometimes conversation. An older woman in the coffee shop accepted her flower. About five minutes later, she asked what I was working on which led to a discussion about my first book. Her husband left to browse the stacks, and I ended up sitting with her for about twenty minutes. We had a meaningful conversation about life, death, and sorrow. Her daughter's husband had committed suicide two years earlier, and her daughter was just coming out on the other side. Her story touched me

so much, that I went out to my car to get a copy of my book and gifted it to her to share with her daughter. I hope that some of my stories made them smile, see that I also came out on the other side after losses in my life.

The last flower went to a young mom in the Children's Section. When I offered her the flower, her face completely lit up. She said, "You just made my day." Pointing to her son, who appeared to have some special needs, she continued, "He had a good doctor appointment and now this." At this point, her daughter appeared to see what was happening. We chatted a bit, the children wished me a happy birthday. As I was walking away, I heard her say, "That lady just did a really nice thing for us, and we don't even know her." I loved that she used our short interlude as a teachable moment for her children.

I had conflicting feelings about using this as a story. I didn't do it for that reason. It was one of the best things I have ever done, and I will definitely do something similar again. I decided to share the story because I strongly believe that life can be changed by a moment or a chance interaction. I think God connects us with people without our knowing it, and there is a reason for it.

I will never forget this birthday and the garden of flowers that I planted for strangers.

> "Wherever there is a human being, there is an opportunity for kindness."
>
> — SENECA, ROMAN PHILOSOPHER

Plant a garden to bloom in the hearts of others. The seeds you sow will result in a harvest that you may never see, but it will be magnificent.

A WHOLE OTHER COUNTRY

I WANTED to share some more sights, tastes, and adventures from...wait for it...Texas, It's a Whole Other Country. I loved that slogan used to draw tourists to the state of Texas. They were not bragging or exaggerating. Texas is a big place with big sights, big food, big boots, big Stetsons, and big water.

Trying to atone for our Panda Express lunch which was our first meal in Texas we were searching for something more culturally appropriate on our last day in the great state of Texas. Heading north, looking to grab lunch, we saw a sign advertising a restaurant called Black's Barbecue. We decided to go for it. When we arrived, signs inside told the story about this family restaurant, open since 1932 (how bad can it be?), and that current Pitmaster, Kent Black, was a third-generation pitmaster. I am hungry and getting excited about some great barbecue. Black's did not disappoint!!

The place was raucous, crowded and definitely a "make new friends kind of place." The side dishes are served buffet-style, so you choose what you want, and then proceed to the purveyors of the main attraction. Choose whatever you want, ribs, brisket, pulled pork, chicken, and anything else they may have slow-smoked and barbecued. Smelled like heaven and the meal was phenomenal. We quickly made friends with the family sitting next to us and had a wonderful time.

One of the side dishes was a pecan pie cobbler. Are you kidding me? This adventure just kept getting better and better!! I was very excited as I love pecan pie and helped myself to a generous portion. As we neared the dessert portion of our meal, I decided we needed ice cream to top off the cobbler. I went back to the front of the restaurant and requested ice cream for two. I thought it would be soft serve, but they handed me two of the plastic containers of ice cream. "Okay," I said to myself, "I bet this is Texas's famous ice cream, Blue Bell." As I approached our table, I was reading the label on the ice cream. It was not Texas Blue Bell ice cream, but it was Iowa's renowned Blue Bunny ice cream!!! Now my day is perfect, the Iowa connection that we always find when we travel, today is Blue Bunny ice cream from LeMars, Iowa.

Wells Blue Bunny recently acquired an East coast competitor. This means that Wells Blue Bunny now employs 3,800 people and produces 200 million gallons of ice cream annually. We do it big in Iowa too!!

If you are like me, my brain says salad, but my stomach autocorrects it to ice cream. Sugar cone, waffle cone, in a dish, regular cone, ice cream is flexible, but always tasty!! Stand up comedienne, Wendy Liebman incorporates exercise into this tasty treat, "I go running when I have to. When the ice cream truck is doing sixty."

Take someone you love to the ice cream shop, and make some memories.

Take someone to Texas, and have Iowa ice cream. Chase the ice cream truck and get a double-dip cone!! There's always room for ice cream!!

SONG OF THE SEA

ON MY MOST recent trip to Florida, I spent many hours admiring and reveling in the sights and sounds of the Gulf of Mexico. The ocean is ever-changing; a mercurial, wild, whimsical and mysterious being. The exuberance of the waves bringing to the beach the riches of the sea.

Depending on the tide, often enormous piles of shells are deposited, fresh and ready for the beachcombers to add to their collection. This year on our beach, there is a secret shell fairy. An early riser evidently walks the beach, collects shells, and then leaves them in a nice pile for people to take. Every day, like clockwork, they mysteriously appear near the grassy area that connects us to the beach.

Of course, the sunshine reflecting off the water and the cornflower blue skies are the images that come to mind when we think of the beach and the ocean. However, the cloudy, stormy, foggy days have their own unique seascape for the viewer's enjoyment. The fog rising off the ocean in the early morning, as the sky turns from gray to blue is exquisite.

Part of the definition of a symphony is "a full orchestra." The sound of the waves crashing the beach is indeed a full orchestra. It is music to my ears, and balm to my soul. To wake and sleep by the sea is indeed a magnificent occurrence.

> "You only need to stand near the ocean to feel the power of the universe and a closeness to the one who created it."
>
> — MERMAID MUSINGS

All of nature gives me the sense of being closer to the Master who painted the skies, the flowers, the waters and all of creation, but the ocean has a special pull on my heart.

CHAPTER V
POTPOURRI

"Potpourri Disclaimer: this is a nice way of labeling the stories that didn't fit in any other chapters…"

— LORI LACINA, AUTHOR

COFFEE SHOP POETRY

Sitting at the table
Watching people watching me.
Giving them a label.
Do they label me?

Lonely man,
Table for one.
Woman friends
Making amends.
Mom & menagerie
Just passing through.

Baristas chatting while
Back and forth,
Forth and back.
Busy hands
Granting demands.
Taking money
Making money.

Hot coffee
Cold coffee
Crunchy cold coffee
Aroma of coffee
Tea for one or three.

Wondering how much longer
I'll be sitting here typing,
Thinking, pondering, and gazing.
Hoping to write something amazing.

THE MYSTERY OF THE POPPY SEED CAKE

SOME YEARS ago friends and I had a recipe for making poppy seed cake that was easy and quite tasty. I hadn't made it for a long time, for a variety of reasons. One day, I started thinking about it and wanted to make one. I went to my trusty, ever faithful recipe box to procure the recipe and make a cake. Much to my dismay, no poppy seed cake recipe in the cake category. Not that I have ever misfiled anything, but I checked the dessert category next, nope not there. I then proceeded to examine my entire recipe box which is stuffed full of hundreds of recipes. I was sure it had become stuck to another recipe or horror of horrors I had misfiled it. Again, nothing, nada, nowhere, not to be found. Where is Nancy Drew when I need her?

Color me disappointed. As the welfare of the entire planet did not rest on whether I found this recipe or not, I let it go for a while. Randomly asked my brother and a few other people I thought might remember the cake and possibly have the recipe. Still nothing. I was beginning to think I had dreamed up this tasty treat and it never really existed. Yet, I persisted.

Then it came to me!! I remembered that a long-time friend that I had recently reconnected with had given me the recipe, oh so many years ago. I immediately texted her with the request for this elusive recipe. Her response was lukewarm...as in...she didn't remember it...didn't think she would have it...but she would take a look. My tiny flickering light of hope was struggling to hold on. But, being the eternal optimist, I hung in there.

Boy howdy, yikes, gadzooks, eureka and holy smokes!! She found it. She sent me a picture of the recipe card. I looked at it, texted back, asking, "Is that my handwriting?" to which she replied in the affirmative. We were both confused about why the recipe would be in

my handwriting. We came to the conclusion that either she stole it from my recipe box in the dead of night, or that another friend gave us the recipe and I copied it for both of us. The latter made the most sense, being the kind, helpful, friendly, smile in every aisle girl that I am.

Mission accomplished, cake was baked!! It was every bit as good as I remember! After all the angst and drama, I decided I should share the recipe with my readers, so they could see what all the fuss was about!

Poppy Seed CakeOrigin Unknown!

1 white cake mix
1 box instant coconut pudding mix
¼ cup poppy seeds

Mix dry ingredients.

Add:
¼ cup liquid shortening
4 eggs
1 cup hot water

Beat well. Bake in a greased bundt pan for 45 minutes at not quite 350 degrees. If you don't have a bundt pan, loaf pans should work. You might have to watch and adjust the baking time.

Happiness is knowing the cake is in the oven.

JUST SAY NO TO THE EYELINER

I HAVE QUESTIONS...LOTS of questions. Today's question is about a cosmetic product that many women use daily. I am not one of those women. There are many reasons for that, which I will delve into later.

The product is eyeliner. In theory, I understand that it is used to "line" the eye, thereby enhancing the eye to be more noticeable and attractive. In some cultures men wear eyeliner. It is thought to draw attention to the eye, which is the soul of human expression.

Here is where I get into trouble. I can barely put on mascara proficiently. My right eye is no problem, but when I put it on my left eye, it looks like a child applied it some days. Knowing this, would anyone really expect me to be able to draw a black line around my eyes with a pointy object? I think not.

Don't get me wrong, I do see uses for some kinds of liners. Parchment paper for cookie sheets, newspapers for litter boxes and bird cages are all good. Lining in certain articles of clothing is very nice. Lining up at recess, for a concert, the taco truck, all necessary things.

I have great admiration for women who can apply eyeliner correctly, enhancing their natural beauty. Putting on makeup is kind of a ritual and if this works as part of their daily routine, I say good for them.

Holland Roden, American actress, has the perfect words for me: "I'm not a big eye makeup girl unless there's a professional doing it-otherwise I look like I have two black eyes." So, until a makeup artist joins my staff, which is unlikely since the only staff I employ right now, is Amazon Alexa and Hazel, my robot vacuum. They work for free, don't demand time off and are always there for me.

BROOKIES

ON A RECENT FAMILY vacation in July; to "enjoy" the very hot, humid, sweltering, sweaty, stifling and oppressive weather in the great state of Texas, I made an astonishing food discovery. No, not fantastic, out of this world barbeque or Mexican, they certainly have that, but a delightful, delectable dessert. (Did I mention how warm it is here? There is not even a word for it!)

It all began with the need to feed five teenagers, and five adults in a quick and easy manner, that would not disrupt the party preparations in the house of the host family. So we loaded everyone up and headed to a deli down here, called McAllisters. It boasts a wonderful menu of tasty sandwiches, Texas-sized spuds with all the toppings, soups and salads. Everyone ordered and enjoyed their lunch.

Surprisingly, as often happens, some of us thought we needed a little something sweet to finish off our lunch. We got an assortment of baked goods to share, and that's when the life-changing event occurred. We discovered "brookies!" Brookies are a wonderful combination of brownies and cookies. Genius!! Two great desserts in one!! Basically, they are a layer of cookie dough with a layer of brownie batter on top and baked. We were very excited about this, and I immediately began research to find recipes for this new discovery!!

Much to my delight, I found several and can't wait to try it out.

There can never be too much dessert in the world! Share a little sweetness in the form of a dessert today, with someone you love!! Be a brookie in a world full of brownies…

RED OR BLUE

IF YOU HAVE political leanings and know whether you live in a red or blue state, that is not where I am going! I, in fact, live in a purple state, politically speaking, which is very confusing! When did we start thinking of our states in color? Are there high definition states, and low definition states? But once again, off-topic!! I am thinking about the colors themselves and associated objects and emotions.

RED	BLUE
Fire engine	Ocean
Hearts	Sky
Sunsets	Indigo Buntings
Anger	Serenity
Hair	Cool/Cold
Sunshine	Clouds
Hot/Warm	Bluebirds
Cardinals	Ice
Foxes	Butterfly
Love	Reflections
Sunrises	Indifference
Roses	Midnight
Fire	Melancholy
Strawberries	Ennui

I am extremely fond of all the nuances of the color blue. Cerulean, navy, midnight, aquamarine, azure, cobalt, sapphire, royal, and ultramarine are all shades of blue. There are many more, but I was trying to avoid getting into the green and purple hues of blue.

It is much harder to name shades of red without entering the pink and purple ranges. Here are some words that mean red to me: ruby, raspberry, wine, magenta, burgundy, cherry, and crimson.

I find it fascinating observing what colors people are drawn to and choose for their clothing, paint, cars, etc. Disclaimer: No offense intended if I say something negative about a color you like!! Each to his own. Wouldn't it be a very boring world if we all liked the same things? Watch the movie, *The Stepford Wives,* if you haven't. Very scary!! When I see a particularly hideous car or house, for example, baby poop green or neon orange, I think to myself; I hope they got a good price on that. Beauty is indeed in the eye of the beholder.

I personally am drawn to jewel tones, reds, deep pinks, purples, and blues. I have a fair complexion, have brown eyes and dark blonde hair (depending on the week). If I wear neutral colors, particularly beige, I disappear. It is like camouflage for me. Come to think of it, maybe I should keep some beige clothing on hand for those days I want to dash into Hy-Vee early in the morning before I have prepared myself properly for public appearances!! I may be onto something...stay tuned.

Take a look at your own choice of colors, what they mean to you. I feel happier and more confident when I am wearing certain colors. Identify those colors that appeal to you emotionally and physically. Use them to your advantage!!

Celerie Kemble, a Palm Beach designer/decorator said, "There's a reason we don't see the world in black and white." We have been gifted all these beautiful colors from the One who paints the sunsets and the rainbows. Embrace the colors in your soul, live your life in vivid strokes of color and share yourself with the world.

OLD OR BOLD?

Society labels me as old,
I prefer to think I am bold.
Those folks I must scold.

Inside, I am the same me
I have always wanted to be.
I wish all the others could see.

With great age, comes many rewards.
There are lots of things to move towards.
No regrets, don't look back, always forward.

I have lived more years than I have left.
I do not feel sad, lonely or bereft.
I am grateful for what I have left.

Embrace your God-given years,
Don't waste time on fears,
Have some beer, make some cheers.

Every moment is a lovely gift,
May those you love give you a lift.
Days are long, years are swift.

Fully live each day.
Show others the way.
Jump into the fray.
Work, love, and play.

EVERY SO OFTEN, I like to try my hand at poetry. It is a different way of using my brain, using words, and having a little fun. May this inspire you to try your hand at a poem, in any form. Write a little ditty in the next card you send or letter that you write.

I felt like expressing my feelings about aging, getting old, becoming a "senior" citizen or any other name one can think of to describe someone who is chronologically gifted, has lived a full life and has so much to offer to their family, friends and the world around them.

The road of life is ever changing, and as we age that road can become more difficult to navigate. But press on we must! When you attain the glorious and grand status of "senior citizen," stay on the road and keep moving forward. The valley has its own beauty, but the view from the mountaintop is spectacular. Climb the mountain, even if you have to stop and catch your breath frequently. Enjoy the view, you have earned it.

GOLDEN ARCHES

I CONSIDER myself to be somewhat of an expert in navigating the drive-up windows at McDonald's. It all started about thirteen years ago. My husband had passed away, the days were long, and I needed places to go. I often just drove around randomly to get out of the house and kill some time. McDonald's had just started offering more than just "regular" coffee. They were advertising iced coffee, with flavors. Part of my driving around ritual became driving through and purchasing an iced coffee to accompany me on my aimless ramble. It was summertime, and I remember worrying that the coffee was seasonal and I wouldn't be able to purchase it when the seasons changed.

I really, really enjoyed the iced coffee...so much so, that I started buying an extra one to take home and have for breakfast the next morning. And so it began...thirteen years later, I am still driving through and bringing iced coffees home for my morning coffee extravaganza. I remember one winter when the wind chills were in the negative 40s or so, the young gentleman handing me my iced coffee, and saying to me, "Really??" It was a comforting ritual at a time when I needed it and still brings me pleasure today.

I would not even venture a guess as to how many times I have been through the drive-through to get an iced coffee. The number is large, hence my claim to be an expert at this activity. Lately, though, I have had to learn a new tactic to complete this ritual in a timely manner. It took me a couple of times, but I've got it now. Here is a time-saving tip for going to the drive-through: If there is more than one lane, never, never get in the line behind the van.

First of all, they are usually ordering enormous quantities of food and drink. This is never easy or quick, it seems to involve lots of conversation with the person taking the order. Also lots of conversations within said van vehicle with the numerous occupants. Then there are the questions...Really? Yes, you can get fries with everything here, move on!!

Unfortunately, it doesn't end there. Paying for the large quantities of food also seems to take forever, again punctuated with a conversation.

I don't know if they are paying with Bitcoin, Euros, Monopoly money, or the Czech Koruna, but it is a transaction that seems too complicated than if they are using American dollars, the customary currency for McDonald's.

Finally, they reach the window where the food is dispensed. Bags upon bags of food, drinks and drink carriers are handed through the van window. Again, there is usually more conversation than I would deem necessary at this point in the transaction. Assuming they are asking for extras, sauce for the nuggets, napkins, salt packets, ketchup packets, straws, and the list goes on…

No offense intended for van owners, just an observation that has occurred multiple times in my vast drive up for iced coffee experience!

For the rest of you, heed my advice, don't choose the lane with the van in it unless you are looking for extra quality time in your vehicle with your audiobook or playlist!!

HOT MILK CAKE

I WAS RUMMAGING through my mom's recipe box and came across this recipe that I had long forgotten. Not a fancy name for a dessert, but fairly descriptive. This is a cake that doesn't need frosting but I leave that to you if you feel you must!! The cake is yummy and I was excited to rediscover this recipe that we used to make. It is back on my radar and will be in my oven soon!! I wanted to share this with you and hope that you will find it a tasty new addition to your collection of recipes.

Hot Milk Cake

Ingredients:
4 eggs 1 tsp vanilla extract
2 cups sugar 1 ¼ cups milk
2 ¼ cups flour 10 Tbsp butter
2 ¼ tsp baking powder

Beat eggs at high speed until thick, about 5 minutes. Gradually add sugar, beating until mixture is light and fluffy. Combine flour and baking powder then add to batter with vanilla and beat at low speed until smooth. In a saucepan, heat milk and butter just until the butter melts, stirring occasionally. Add to batter, beating until combined. Pour into a greased 13-inch by 9-inch baking pan. Bake at 350 degrees for 30-35 minutes or until cake tests done. Cool on a wire rack.

Eat and enjoy this old-fashioned cake. Perfectly acceptable at any meal, and is definitely a breakfast treat!!!

PETER PAN'S GIFT

THE WORD PHILANTHROPY has always struck me as a "toney" word. It seems fancy, high brow and reserved for the wealthy. By definition, it seems notably softer! It means a desire to help others and improve their welfare, usually with a financial contribution. One does not have to be rich to give small donations to worthy causes, every single dollar combines with other donations to help make a difference. I would compare it to the ripple effect achieved when you throw a pebble in a lake.

The idea of philanthropy came to mind after I discovered a very unique and noble philanthropic act. I am guessing you are familiar with the character of Peter Pan. Whatever version you may have read, or seen; animated, stage or movie has timeless magic to entice young and old to enter into Peter's fantasy world. Flying away to Neverland, meeting Tinkerbell, and staying young forever.

Peter Pan came into existence in 1902 in the form of a book by Scottish novelist and playwright, James Barrie or J.M. Barrie.

The original book was titled "The Little White Bird." The book about a young boy who could fly and who would never grow old was an instant favorite. If you read the book, there is a much darker side than what is portrayed by Disney and other modern versions.

As you are reading this rambling prose, I bet you are wondering if I have lost my mind (probably) or my train of thought (it's a short train). I can almost read your thoughts…"She has made some pretty extreme stretches in telling a story, but this one may be her downfall." What does Peter Pan have to do with philanthropy?

This story touched my heart so much I wanted to share it. James Barrie gave the Peter Pan copyright to Great Ormond Street Hospital in London. It is one of the leading children's hospitals in the world, founded in 1852. The royalties from Peter Pan still continue to help the hospital, 80 years after his death. It was indeed the gift that keeps on giving, to a very special cause. One of the stipulations Barrie made, was that the hospital would never reveal how much money they received from these royalties.

How apropos...the boy who would never grow old, will continue to help other children for all eternity. A match made in heaven, or maybe Neverland. As Peter said, "All you need is faith, love and a little Pixie Dust." Of course, a helping hand never hurts either.

So grow up we must, but on the way, we can help others less fortunate. A favorite saying of mine goes something like this, after all, in the end, we are all just walking each other home. So let's take a hand and walk through this world together.

THE MAKING OF A QUILT

MANY PEOPLE HAVE a vague idea of what a quilt is, particularly if they have been gifted with one from someone who loves them. A quilt is basically a blanket with three layers: the top which is usually colorful and pieced (sewn) into a pattern; the middle is cotton batting for warmth and insulations, and the back is the final piece to making a quilt sandwich. These three layers are quilted (sewn) together). Voila! A quilt is born!

Quilts are a part of our American history. They tell stories and show the changes over time in our culture. The quilters of yesteryears saved every scrap of fabric from unusable clothing to be used in a future quilt. They swapped those precious pieces of fabric with friends to obtain different colors. Once in a while, they might be able to purchase a small piece of fabric. Their quilts were made from a necessity to have blankets to keep the family warm. Over time, they were also created and saved for the time a daughter of the family would marry and need quilts for her new household. Women came together to help finish the quilts, conversing, sharing, and stitching. Getting and receiving help. Joining in…

I am blessed to have a double wedding ring quilt that my great-grandmother Ora made. It is full size, with thousands of tiny stitches. It is a work of art and a work of love. I am not sure when she made it, but it has to be close to one hundred years old. The small pieces of fabric clearly represent the clothing from that era. It is a treasure. I was fortunate enough to have her in my life for about twenty years. I remember her with much love, and many of the pearls of wisdom she imparted stay with me today.

I learned recently that 80% of quilters come to quilting because of a loss. That was certainly true in my case, even if that is probably not a very scientifically proven number. I had always been fascinated by quilts and thought I would like to make one. Slight problem with that ambition is that I didn't know how to sew. Never let minor obstacles such as that stop you from trying something. Seven months ago I didn't know how to read music, and I am playing the ukulele like a crazy person! How does the song go, "Ain't no mountain high enough…"

Back to the fascination with quilts. One very long year after my husband died, I was shopping with my brother and his family who were back for Easter. We passed a sewing machine shop. I hesitated and then decided to go in. I talked to the sales clerk about my desire to quilt coupled with my inability to sew. I am sure she was impressed with those credentials. She asked me one question, "Do you think you could sew a straight line?" I answered in the affirmative, thinking to myself, surely even I could manage that. I walked out with a Brother sewing machine, and the rest is history. Ten years later, I am on my third upgraded sewing machine and have made hundreds of quilts.

I have made many new friends while pursuing this new hobby. It didn't take long to discover that quilting is not normally an individual hobby. The quilting community is generous, giving, helpful and willing to mentor a newbie. They use their talents not just for their own quilt needs but for charity and community needs. I know that not all quilters come to the hobby because of a loss. I hope that many come as part of a celebration, needing to make a T-shirt quilt or a new baby quilt or a wedding quilt.

There are a lot of humorous things that are part of quilting. The best is probably quilt pattern names. Let me share a few of the more traditional patterns.

Drunkard's Path	Rail Fence
One Way	Robbing Peter to Pay Paul
Flying Geese	Steps to the Altar
Dutchman's Puzzle	Yankee Puzzle
Birds in the Air	Ohio Star
Friendship Star	Mariner's Compass
Churn Dash	Double Wedding Ring
Grandmother's Choice	Broken Dishes
Bachelor's Puzzle	Confederate's Rose
Nine Patch	Log Cabin

Phylicia Rashad, American actress, singer and director, put it this way, "Anytime women come together with a collective intention, it's a powerful thing. Whether it's sitting down making a quilt, in a kitchen preparing a meal, in a club reading the same book, or around the table playing cards, or planning a birthday party, when women come together with a collective intention, magic happens."

When women join their hearts and minds together, I believe they can do anything. They can move mountains.

Join a group of women, make a quilt, read a book, share your thoughts and ideas. Wonder Woman is not just a fictional character, it is a mindset. Make something happen. Make your life, and the world a better place. It can all start with something as simple as joining in.

WHERE'S THE HAM IN MY SOUP?

I CAN NEVER DECIDE if potato soup or chili is my favorite soup of the season. They are so different and both are so yummy. Chili is much less labor-intensive so it is great for those busy winter days. My mom used to make potato soup, but she didn't put ham in it. It was simply potato soup. My late husband grew up with ham in potato soup, and thought it was more of a "meal." Translation: Iowa farm boys need meat to make it a meal!! Hence, the transformation of my soup!!

Potato Soup (with ham!)

Ingredients:
5 # of potatoes
1 onion
1 stick of butter
Diced ham (Amount is personal preference)
A 32-ounce bag of frozen mixed vegetables (California mix which contains cauliflower, broccoli, and carrots.)
Velveeta cheese diced (I know, not real cheese, but it melts into the soup so nicely)
Milk

Directions:

Peel and cut the potatoes in quarters. Boil them in a large pot until almost done. Add the frozen vegetables and continue to cook. When the vegetables are done, drain the water. Add the stick of butter and mash the potatoes and vegetables to the desired consistency. Add ham, diced Velveeta cheese. Add milk, again to desired thickness. Continue to cook on a very low heat so the milk doesn't scald. Stir frequently until the soup is at the desired temperature.

This soup can be very flexible if you are creative and want to make changes. I am not a gourmet cook by any stretch of the imagination but I like to share the simple recipes I grew up with. This is tasty and a pretty hearty meal by itself.

Cooking with love is food for the heart. Sharing food you have made with your own hands with those you care about is one of the most special things you can give.

> "Homemade with love. In other words, I licked the spoon and kept using it."

— SPICY GOULASH

Make some soup, bake some pie, share some love. It really is that simple.

♥ ♥ ♥

MISSION IMPOSSIBLE — MY DAILY LIFE

THERE ARE ALWAYS things in life that are hard to accomplish. Some are physically hard, some are emotionally hard, some are circumstantially hard. Life is a road with potholes, with bridges to cross, rivers to ford, mountains to climb, envelopes to push, glass ceilings to break...well, you get the point. These obstacles do not become easier as you get older. I would like to share some of my daily obstacles. I don't want your sympathy, but maybe I can help a little if you share any of these painful episodes.

I was doing last-minute packing recently for a weekend trip. I realized I needed a lip balm, so I proceeded to the lip balm department at my house. I found a new one and decided to get it open so it would be at the ready if I had a lip balm emergency. Well, the emergency turned out to be opening the lip balm. That microscopic paper tag that is supposed to allow you to pull it and unseal the lip balm was not my friend. After several unsuccessful tries, I went to Plan B. (Note-my kids and grandkids should stop reading here) I went to the kitchen drawer and got out a knife. I relentlessly attacked that lip balm seal with my knife, and voila, I was able to get it open. I am a problem solver. Although my family thinks I shouldn't have knives at my disposal.

Then there was the water bottle episode. I purchased a case of water bottles, generic label. Great price, water is water...or is it? Water is not as valuable when you can't drink it, because you can't get the lid off. I literally was cutting my hand trying to twist the lid off. In case you think it was just me, the weak link, it was not. My gentleman friend had the same problem, as did a number of friends who also partook in the great deal. Sometimes one of those rubber jar grippers would work, sometimes pliers were required. Unfortunately, I don't usually carry those with me on my bicycle...which was where I generally needed to drink the water. Clearly I had not planned for every eventuality!

After a number of injurious incidents, I gave up on the water. I am not a quitter but as Kenny Rogers sang in the song "The Gambler," You have to know when to hold 'em and know when to fold 'em. Good advice.

I could go on, but I think this is enough angst to share with you today. Life is fraught with challenges, but unless it can be fixed with duct tape or WD40, I am not your girl. Somedays, you just have to do whatever it takes to survive.

SHRINKFLATION

SHRINKFLATION, as I understand it, is the unfortunate practice of reducing the size of a product without a corresponding reduction in price. I have observed this before, but recently it affected my personal health and welfare, so I feel I must speak out.

I wouldn't complain, but I feel like an injured party. Well, to be perfectly clear, when I am injured, the bandaids add insult to injury, literally. Has anyone else noticed that no matter what size you purchase, the center gauze pad is almost invisible?? I can't even see it without my glasses on. Some of the sizes have a center cushion that is so small if your injury is that small you really don't need a bandaid. Not only is it smaller in size, but it also is not nearly as cushioned. I don't think I am imagining this trend. I also don't think my various cuts and scrapes are necessarily that much larger than the normal person. There I go again, comparing myself to normal people. It's a bad habit. I am working on it.

Maybe you have noticed this trend in other products. The five-pound bags of sugar I used to buy are no longer five pounds. Do the manufacturers and retailers think we won't notice? I still say I need five pounds of sugar on my grocery list, but that is not really what I am purchasing. I can live with the four-pound sugar bag, but I am struggling with the miniature gauze wound pads.

I hope that some of you are sympathetic to my cause. I would hate to think I am the only one out here noticing and struggling with these very important issues. Some of you may think I need a hobby to occupy my time. Unfortunately, I have a number of hobbies that do not quell my penchant for pondering and juggling these earth-shattering questions. Maybe that's why Curious George was my favorite childhood book…

A BOWL OF LORI'S CHILI

THE CHILLY DAYS of autumn and the frigid temperatures of a Heartland winter are the perfect backdrops for making soup. Warms you from the inside out, feeds your body and your soul! There are thousands of recipes for chili, and mine is nothing special, but my friends and family enjoy it. It is simple to make, no fancy ingredients or techniques to learn!! Add more or less of any ingredient, I judge what to add by how it looks, and when the crockpot is full!

Lori's Chili

Turn on the crockpot (large crockpot) and start the process!!

Brown 2 pounds of ground beef in a skillet. Add diced onion while it is cooking. Drain. Dump in crockpot when browned.

Dump (technical cooking term) the following ingredients in the crockpot:

- 46 ounce can of your favorite tomato juice
- 2-3 29 ounce cans of diced tomatoes
- 1-2 cans of original Rotel
- 3 cans of light/dark kidney beans or chili beans
- 2-3 T of chili powder (I start with one heaping, and keep adding while tasting throughout the day)
- 1-2 little scoops of sugar later in the day, cuts the bitterness of the beans

Cook in a crockpot or slow cooker for at least 4 hours, I cook mine all day to enjoy the aromas and let the flavors really blend together. I also make homemade cornbread to enjoy with the chili.

Serve with the following add-ons: oyster crackers, chopped green onion, shredded cheese, black olives, and sour cream.

In my opinion, the chili is even better the second day, and I often freeze it in quart freezer bags.

"Chili is not so much food as a state of mind. Addictions to it are formed early in life and the victims never recover. On blue days in October, I get this passionate yearning for a bowl of chili, and I nearly lose my mind."

— Margaret Elizabeth Cousins, Irish-Indian Suffragist, and Theosophist.

I, too am yearning for chili, after writing out this recipe, while I work in the very cold coffee shop I frequent. The outdoor temperature today does not lend itself to chili, but perhaps I will ignore the inappropriate season and think about making chili. Bon appetit!

FOOLED BY SWEDISH RICE

I HAD BEEN "DATING" (if that is what you call it at my age) my most significant other, Mr. Verne for some time, and I had heard him mention on more than one occasion a favorite dish of his called, "Swedish Rice." He is Swedish so it made sense. He extolled the virtues of this rare and mouth-watering delicacy on many occasions.

I never asked a lot of questions. I was glad he was embracing his cultural heritage from his dad who was the product of Swedish parents.

Then one day his sister came to visit, and she brought...wait for it...Swedish Rice for him. Saints be praised and give thanks for the blessing of this much-heralded dish. As an inquisitive person, as most writers are, I needed to investigate this special delicacy.

Color me disappointed. What I thought was a special secret recipe, brought over on a boat from Sweden by Mr. Verne's grandparents was the very same dish I grew up eating, that my mom called Rice Pudding.

What a let-down! I felt cheated and disappointed!! Plus, I couldn't believe that is what he had been talking about all that time!!

My mom made this dish fairly frequently, considering my dad would not eat rice. He spent two years in Japan while he was in the Army and evidently had eaten all the rice in one lifetime that he was going to. Rice would not have been a normal dish for the Iowa farm boy that's for certain. Very little red meat, mashed potatoes, and fresh milk straight from the cow in Japan.

My brother, Randy, loved this dish more than any of us. It was fine, and I had no objection to it but didn't have the love for it that he did.

I feel I should share this recipe, and if you decide to make it, you can call it whatever you want!!

Mom's Rice Pudding

Bring 2 cups of rice to a boil in 3 ½ cups of water. Then simmer on low heat until the water is gone. Put rice in an ovenproof bowl with one quart of milk. ½ cup of sugar, and a little vanilla. Cover the top lightly with cinnamon. Stir together. Bake at 325 degrees for about one hour, but do check on it before then. It is done when all the milk is cooked in. Don't overcook and let it get too dry.

I have heard that some folks put raisins in the rice pudding. I shudder at the mere thought. There are so many things wrong with this...just like ruining oatmeal cookies by hiding raisins in them for the unsuspecting cookie lover to find.

Mitch Hedberg, an American stand-up comedian said this: "Rice is great if you're really hungry and want to eat two thousand of something." Well put, Mr. Hedberg, just don't put any raisins in mine!

SATURDAY MORNING COCKTAILS

Saturday morning...time to relax with the morning news and cup of coffee. Nowhere to be, easy kind of morning...or so you would think.

Minding my own business, starting my day. I jump in the shower and feel like something isn't right. Pain near my breastbone feels like the daily medications I took didn't go down the right way. Done with the shower, drink some water, that doesn't help. The pain is increasing and I am very uncomfortable. Recognition strikes...I have had this pain before.

Urgent Care, clear the decks, I am on my way. I checked in online and headed out. I know what this is, and I also know the hoops I will jump through to get relief. I am fairly certain I am having a bad acid reflux attack. Unfortunately, the symptoms are similar to heart attack symptoms for women. They administer an EKG as a rule-out, it looks great and the doctor agrees with my diagnosis. If they would just let me write my own prescriptions in these cases, it sure would save me time! I am very in tune with my body, and I rarely miss an episode of Grey's Anatomy. I think I could do a tracheotomy with a ballpoint pen, I have seen it done on TV. Confidence and calm are the key ingredients to acting in an emergency situation.

Feeling productive now, it's only 10:00 AM, and I have had an EKG and a lidocaine cocktail. As I told them the first time this happened, had I known they served cocktails, I would have been in much sooner. The nurse walked in with mine saying, "Drinks on the house." Love medical professionals who have a sense of humor! Drank the aforementioned cocktail, which provides very quick relief. It numbs your throat and all the way down. The downside is, no drinking or eating anything else for an hour since your throat is numb...choking or aspiration is not recommended or enjoyable.

After a short observation period, I am on my way, proud owner of a prescription for more lidocaine so I can mix my own cocktail if necessary. Thankful for the world-class medical care where I live, and the professionals who provide the care when I need it.

THIRTEEN RANDOM FACTS ABOUT THE AUTHOR

1. My late husband looked like Elvis Presley when he was young, and his classmates called him the "Elvis of St. Patrick's," the Catholic school he attended.
2. I have met two former Presidents and had my picture taken with them: President Ronald Reagan and President Gerald Ford.
3. I taught classes at Kirkwood Community College for several years as an adjunct professor.
4. Dream Job #1--Talk show host
5. I met my husband at a bar called The Red Stallion.
6. I wanted to go to law school.
7. Three friends and I may have been asked never to return to the Hotel Fort Des Moines when we were in high school.
8. My brain is like an iPod on a shuffle playlist.
9. I fractured two vertebrae in my back when I was a senior in high school during gym class.
10. For my 5th birthday, I asked for and received a cowboy holster with guns and a hula skirt...and wore them together.
11. I love random facts, especially in a list.
12. Dream job #2-- own a bookshop which would be called, "Once Upon a Book."
13. Thirteen is my favorite number.

HAVE some fun making your own random facts lists. Share with family and friends. This could be a great party game. Groucho Marx said, "If you're not having fun, you're doing something wrong."

CHAPTER VI

ALPHABET SOUP

This short chapter is an extension of some pages in my first book.

I started sharing fun words beginning with each letter of the alphabet. Many readers commented they really enjoyed the word pages. So the letters I used here are the ones that didn't make the first book. Far be it from me to leave any alphabet letters out in the cold! There are only 26 and we need them all.

> "I'm intrigued that the same letters from the alphabet are used in the word silent and the word listen. Perhaps it's evidence that the most important part of listening involves remaining silent."

> — ROBERT HERJAVEC, CANADIAN BUSINESS MAN, INVESTOR, CELEBRITY ON SHARK TANK.

for C3—! Alone we word in Silence

PS 62

Jim 2021

THE LETTER "A"

I FEEL LIKE SHARING TODAY, and since there is no adult version of show and tell that I know about, and would be welcomed at, this page will have to do!

My love of words leaks out of everything I write. The English language has so many beautiful and descriptive words, and it is so easy to have the habit of making the easy choice when speaking or writing, rather than working at it. Guess this goes for life too, but that can wait for another day. Today is about my favorite words that begin with the letter "A," which makes the title of this essay appropriate if not very subtle…

Alchemy
Abubble
Alluring
Ardent
Abuzz
Ambidextrous
Alliteration
Askance
Atingle
Amber
Atwinkle
Allegory
Alabaster

This quote from Ludwig Wittgenstein, a 20th-century philosopher has great meaning for me: "The limits of my language are the limits of my world."

NUMBER FOUR

It's okay to be number four. Not everyone has to be number one. So today's shout out is to the letter "D." The fourth letter in our alphabet. "D" is a part of many delightful and delicious words!! Here are some of my favorites:

Decorum	Deportment
Daft	Dither
Dabble	Damsel
Dazzle	Dizzy
Dapper	Daisy
Dandelions	Dashing
Diaries	Debunk
Diligent	Decorous
Demerits	Demure
Diamonds	Diaphanous
Dalliance	Diligent
Diabolical	Dainty

I am dizzy with delight dabbling in the dazzling world of "D"s!

Aware, am I, that some readers who know me would think I don't know much about words like decorum and deportment. They are wrong.

Defending myself in advance, am I!!

Have fun today diligently using some dashing "D" words in your conversations. You will dazzle your friends, family, acquaintances possibly and random strangers on the street!

"E"ASY DOES IT

EVENTUALLY, you must have estimated that I would have to share words that belong to the letter "E" with you. Continuing this from my first book, because I must not leave out any letters. I would never insult the alphabet that way!! Favorite "E" words coming your way…

Enigma	Elegant
Exotic	Endear
Erstwhile	Euchre
Eternal	Eloquent
Edify	Ecumenical
Exquisite	Equanimity
Eloquent	Etch
Eleven	Empire
Elude	Egg
Eerie	Edgy
Ebb	Eatery

On your journey today, edify your friends using some wonderful "E" words. Ask them to join your elegant and exotic empire and play eleven games of euchre at your favorite ecumenical eatery. It could turn out to be edgy and eerie!!

JUST M

Alphabet soup again!! The letter "M" is truly a wonderful letter. It is the 13th letter in the alphabet, and 13 is my lucky number. 13's have always popped up in my life in one way or another. Besides that, there are so many yummy words that begin with "M."

Modicum	Mutiny
Megalomaniac	Merriment
Malarkey	Majestic
Myriad	Minx
Macaroons	Mollycoddle
Magic	Mimic
Madcap	Malaprop
Macrame	Malinger
Meatloaf	Marauder
Meld	Magi
Mash	Moolah
Maze	Mauve

What fun there is to be had with today's words!! Imagine a madcap minx enjoying a macaroon amidst the merriment, marauders, and mutiny! Don't be a malinger and expect to be mollycoddled!!

Decorate your conversation or journaling today with descriptive, evocative words!!

NOTEWORTHY N

TIME TODAY, to take note of number fourteen in the alphabet, the nimble and nifty letter "N." It is a very nice and helpful consonant that really needs no introduction. Probably the most used word that "N" is the captain of is the word "no." I ask you, faithful readers, where would we be without the word, "no?"

Without further ado, let me share some of my favorite words that begin with the noble letter "N."

Nestled	Nab
Nincompoop	New-fangled
Novelty	Nifty
Nuzzle	Nimble
Novelty	Neatnick
Nibble	Nonsense
Nerd	Niggle
Noodles	Nudge
Nickel	Nesting
Numbskull	Naughty

Now that you (k)now all these novel and nerdy "N" words, don't neglect to use them whether necessary or not regardless of any naysayers that you have to nudge.

Words are so important to me, and so important in everyday life. Words can inspire, motivate, delight and thrill. Use your words well and kindly.

"You never know when a moment and a few sincere words can have an impact on a life."

— ZIG ZIGLAR, AMERICAN MOTIVATIONAL SPEAKER

AN ODE TO O

TIME FOR RECOGNIZING another friendly letter in the alphabet. I don't have any favorites, they are all special in their own way. O is an important member of a small group-the vowel. The vowels are an elite club, and attention must be paid to them. There aren't very many of them, but they are mighty! Here follows a random list of "O" words that I am particularly fond of.

Obtuse	Oleander
Oasis	Octogenarian
Ocelot	Occult
Oceanic	Obscure
Obligatory	Oak
Oneself	Ode
Ow	Oaf
Oops	Ouchie
Oinks	Onyx
Oblique	Opaque
Oblivion	Oblivious
Ochre	Orange

Entertain yourself and your friends with lots of "O" words today. You can easily work them into the conversation. Something like, I saw an oblivious octogenarian with an ouchie, carrying a stem of oleander while walking an ocelot. See how easily that could be worked into an everyday conversation! Have fun and I wish you a day that is not ordinary!

Q IS FOR ...

LUCKY YOU, I still haven't run out of words to share with you, even if you were wishing I had! So today's letter is Q, which is a pretty elite group of words. There aren't that many words that start with Q, so these words are pretty special

Quiche	Quartz
Quaver	Quake
Quarts	Queasy
Quiver	Quirky
Quip	Quicken (not the software!)
Quacked	Quaffed
Quanked	Quizzed
Quibble	Quixotic

Now that is one very fine group of words. Try working some of them into your conversation today. For example, She made a quirky quiche with quarts of eggs today while quibbling with her daughter who was queasy and quanked after her overnight work session.

Trust me, people will be spellbound. Use your words carefully.

Words have the power to amuse, to give peace, to invite, to share the love and to hurt. Share your words to make your little corner of the world a better place.

"R" YOU READY FOR THIS?

IN HONOR of my brother Randy, who is having heart surgery today, I will share some of my favorites "R" words!

Rapscallion	Resounding
Rucksack	Rhapsody
Rick rack	Riotous
Rascal	Ridiculous
Rustling	Rambunctious
Revelry	Regale
Royal	Relevant
Repudiate	Romance
Radiant	Rainbow
Refreshing	Respite
Reap	Regal

Today would be a great day to regale your friends and family with riotous and refreshing words to really make them relate to your ridiculous revelry and the rick rack on your rucksack.

TIME FOR T

INDULGING myself today by sharing more of my favorite words. Today's show and tell will feature the letter "T." T is the 20th letter in the alphabet and a strong member of the team.

Here we go…

Tangy	Tickled
Tantalize	Thrive
Timeless	Taco
Tootsie	Tux
Twinkle	Tango
Tempest	Tamale
Tubular	Tardy
Tympanic	Tactile
Text (the noun)	Tart

Troy and Todd thrived on tangy tacos and tamales even though it made them tardy for their tantalizing tango lessons.

Thought for the day: It might take two to tango, but it's also okay to dance on your own! Dance even if nobody else hears the music...

U-NIQUE

MY LOVE of words and letters of the alphabet continues with the quiet, uncelebrated and unassuming letter "U." I have become fond of the letter "U' in the last eight months since I began playing the ukulele.

The ukulele has brought me much joy, a feeling of accomplishment and learning. That joy has overflowed onto the letter 'U." Here are some of my favorite words that begin with this late in the alphabet letter!

Unique	Undiminished
Unabashed	Uplifted
Utter	Urbane
Unflappable	Ukulele
Undone	Unfazed
Ubiquitous	Ultimate
Umbrage	Utensil
Uncle	Ulterior
Umpteenth	Ultra-violet
Uptown	Urchin
UFO	Ukuladies

The majority of "U" words begin with the prefix "un." I find this amusing because many of these words we do not use in ordinary conversation without the prefix. I have never called someone flappable, for instance!

Disclaimer: Ukuladies may or may not be a word, but it was the term my friend Debby and I coined when we started our ukulele lessons. Keep an eye out for our first CD...

Wishing you a day where you are uplifted, urbane, undiminished with unflappable confidence and are not accosted by ornery urchins.

WONDERING ABOUT W

WONDERING, as I am wandering, if you are as fond of the letter "W" as I am...I try not to play favorites among the letters of the alphabet, but "W" has some pretty wild and whimsical words to offer!! Hold on to your seat, and take a look!!

Wax	Wane
Whole-hearted	Waft
Whimsical	Whizbang
Wheedle	Wizard
Wordsmith	Whopping
Wildebeest	Wild
Whither	Wither
Wheelie	Whipped
Whack	Whiz
Waves	Wacky
Waif	Wahoo
Wobble	Waffle
Waggle	Wallaby

Those of you familiar with my work, are wailing and whining, thinking enough with the words already!! As I have stated from here to Pluto and back, I encourage diversity in word choice, in hopes of "dressing up" our daily conversations and trying to use less generic words in conversation or writing when we have so many choices. So here is wishing you a whizbang, wild and wacky day. Get out the bicycle and do a wheelie but don't run into any wobbling wizards or waifs. Okay... I am stopping now. No wavering here.

WHY?

ONE MUST ASK THE QUESTION, and then, of course, there is an answer. It is time to explore another alphabet letter. I wouldn't say this letter is an afterthought, but it is the second to last letter in the parade of 26.

I was not sure I could find as many interesting words starting with the letter "Y." and I can't tell you "Y" I thought that, but I was wrong!! A very dandy set of words to ponder.

Yearn	Yokel
Yank	Yarn
Yacht	Yummy
Yaks	Yodel
Yelp	Yacks
Youth	Yearling
Yesteryear	Yammer
Yap	Yawn
Yowl	Yahoo
Yankee	Yardstick

Pretty juicy bunch of words, if I do say so myself. How much fun can you have working these into a daily conversation?? I yearn for yesteryear when you could yank a yokel from his yacht for yodeling, yowling, yammering, and consorting with Yankees. Your friends, families, and co-workers will be stunned at the new turn your vocabulary has taken as you sprinkle some of these words into your next conversation.

Carol Burnett, beloved American comedienne said, "Words, once they are printed have a life of their own." It seems safe to say the same about the spoken word. Expand your vocabulary, use all your words, and use them carefully.

❤ ❤ ❤

'the lonke'
the Song —
'MacArthur Parke'
(64)

'Georgia,
Porgie'
(62)

POSTSCRIPT

Hello!! Just a note from me!! I hope you have enjoyed this book.

It came from my heart, my life and my experiences. It isn't Shakespeare, just the ramblings of an Iowa girl who likes to write.

I would like to thank my readers as it is you who made me an author!! Without you I am simply a writer longing for an audience!! I hope my words have meant something to you, made you think, made you laugh and cry about this life we live.

If you haven't seen my first book, "Mama Said There'd Be Days Like This," I hope you will pick it up. It is a daily reading of reflections and stories. If you enjoyed "Extra Sprinkles," I think you will like it.

Until we meet again…"Let the rivers clap their hands, Let the mountains sing together for joy." Psalm 98:8

May the moon rise in a clear, crisp sky filled abundantly with stars. Time to sleep, dream and refresh ourselves for tomorrow. Day is done. Night has come. Sweet dreams.

Lori Lacina

217

ACKNOWLEDGEMENTS

My brothers, Randy and Bill Detweiler, my first friends and partners in crime, thanks for your support.

Ellie Firestone, Fiverr-who once again guided me through the technical issues of book publishing, and who is responsible for the interior look of the book.

Morgan Krehbiel, book cover designer extraordinaire, two times in a row! Her valuable input and artistry are amazing.

Beta readers, Sue Evans, Cathy DeValk and Verne Nelson. Their content input and proofreading were second to none.

Prairie Lights-Iconic Iowa City independent book store who sells my book and has provided a place to drink coffee, contemplate and write for authors too numerous to mention.

To all those who wonder as they read, if I am writing about you...I am.